XY Theory

The Dangerous Test

How Relationships End *Before* They Begin.

John K. Jacob, Ph.D.

XULON PRESS

XY Theory
The Dangerous Test
by John K. Jacob, PhD

Printed in the United States of America

ISBN 9781624199561

www.xulonpress.com

In memory of my father.

Contents

Introduction

*I*t was a whirlwind romance by all standards. She was gorgeous, smart, sophisticated, and said all the right things. She loved the movies Joe liked, and his favorite music was on her iPod. She absolutely dreamed of living in the very places that he dreamed of. She wanted two kids but agreed that three kids or even one would suffice, if that's what he wanted. She had an accent that always caught his attention, as he had one himself—evidence of the 15 years he'd spent in London. Now, New York was his home. He told her she had eyes like a doe, and she did. They met through mutual friends, as many couples do, or at least as they used to before the advent of Internet dating. But when he first saw her, he did a double take and then struggled to find the first words of introduction, a fact she brought up quite often. When Joe spoke to friends and family about her, he spoke in glowing terms of a perfect woman who liked everything he liked and, most of all was really into him. A few cautioned him to be careful, but he was not. He went full-speed ahead, and when he saw the red flags, he ripped them off the flag poles and threw them away.

Joe knew I was already in the final stages of perfecting a test, a personality test that could actually tell whether any relationship would flourish or flounder, succeed or fail, even before that relationship began. In fact, my bold claim is that you need not have met or personally communicated with your love interest to assess their compatibility—because the XY (Relationship) Personality Test™ could do that for you, even from a distance. You can know within seconds whether he or she is the one for you. Joe knew the questions on the test, too. After all, he and I were good friends, and I kept him informed of my research findings every step of the way. So he should have known better. The least he could've done was run through a mental checklist in his head so he could ask a few useful questions, but she swept him off his feet and he refused to assess her personality. Later, he admitted, "I thought we had *so* much in common."

Having encouraged thousands to take the XY Personality test *before* getting intimate, I knew it was dangerous to do otherwise. But this was Joe's dance with fate. He would rely on what he could *see* instead of what he could *know* if he only took the time to give her the very personality test it took me years to create. But I am getting way ahead of my story.

Many self-help books written in the last three decades, and most of the Internet dating sites, will tell you that you need to have lots in common with your partner—common interests, common goals, similar backgrounds, and similar dispositions—to make it as a couple. As important as those are, in the following chapters of this book and in its companion volume, XY Theory Volume II, I will show you that what we thought for decades was most important, simply is not.

The information you need on how to apply XY Theory to your life will be presented in two volumes. The first introduces you to the theory and all you need to know to identify your personality type. The second book takes the process a step further by teaching you how to apply the theory to your dating and your current relationships. Topics such as getting a commitment, managing conflict, dealing with control issues, and learning how to compromise to effect change will all be covered.

In this book, we will talk about the problems that frustrate most couples. We'll explore why, when we are not dating *deliberately or intentionally* but casually, where we choose a partner at random, we have less than a 1 in 4 chance of choosing a mate who has what we need to make us happy. We'll find out why even after we've found out the reasons why, it's still very difficult to cut our losses and walk away. We'll discuss communication differences and how they affect our relationships and cause emotional disconnection, and difficulty with problem solving. We'll also talk about the factors that lead to sexual disinterest and dissatisfaction. We'll take a look at role overload (or why one partner generally believes it's OK to allow the other to do most of the domestic work), as well as what leads to cheating and other extramarital problems.

You will find that quite often, the obvious problems are not the real problem causing the heartache, and there are other unspoken feelings behind the emotions expressed. Many problems are just symptoms of the real issues. We use words to express what we feel, but we do so using ineffective means that hurt our partners in ways we never intended.

My hope is that as you read this book, you will come to realize that each of us enters a relationship with specific goals and to satisfy unstated needs. It is vital to the relationship that you discover your partner's true intent, real needs, and genuine wants. I believe that at the core of most relationship conflicts is an XY difference that infects or influences how couples handle difficulties. As such, anyone who has experienced problems in a relationship has probably noticed that some issues reoccur. Some are devastating and serious, while other struggles are trivial, and seemingly avoidable.

It's Not the Tea

One man described a fight he had with his wife of 35 years, over how he made her tea. The strange thing is, he had made her tea the same way for 35 years. He would take out her favorite mug and put in two spoons of brown sugar, followed by two bags of Lipton, her favorite brand, then pour the hot water and wait a few minutes. However, he didn't know that *these* minutes of waiting would be different from any others he'd had in 35 years of marriage. He hadn't heard her tiptoe to the kitchen door. He didn't notice her peeping over his shoulder to see what he was doing, and if he had, it would not have mattered. Or so he would have thought. But what ensued was one of the nastiest fights this couple could recall. She asked him if he knew anyone else in the "whole world" that made tea the way he did. He truly didn't know what she was talking about. She insisted that everyone puts the bags in first, hot water next, and then the sugar. He insisted that it didn't matter in what order the items were placed in the cup. Moreover, he had done it that way for 35 years, and she clearly enjoyed the taste because she had never once complained.

I found his account of what happened so incredulous that I had to hear her side of the story, so I asked if she would meet with me. Her account was identical to his except for what she added at the end. She said, "For 35 years I put up with this man never wanting to talk to me, to carry on a conversation with me like we used to before we got married. I'm now convinced this is his nature, his personality. Maybe he can't help who he is. Well, I'm sick of it, and I'm not putting up with him anymore!"

It's the Personality

No, it was not the tea. In fact, it's probably not anything that you've argued about, either. In chapter 1, we'll take a look at why your fate in relationships is often set—even before you've begun to put in years of effort to try to make it work. Then we'll take a look at dangerously disturbing ideas and research in chapter 2. Chapters 3 though 9 will describe X and Y personalities in enough detail so that without a test you can have an idea of what you're dealing with. In order to find a love match that will stand the test of time, you'll need to know which personality you're bringing to the mix. But our goal is to take as much of the guesswork out of forming relationships as possible. We leave nothing to chance. So even if, after getting that far in the book, you have a good sense of who you are and what you need, you're encouraged to read chapters 10 and 11 carefully and get personality tested so you know what you're bringing to the table. It's difficult to get a partner to supply your needs if you're unclear about what those needs are.

Volume II of this book describes XY couples and their conflicts and their struggle to resolve issues, and it offers recommendations and techniques you can use to fix problems in your relationships. It also focuses on how to get your partner to make a commitment and to compromise or change. In the course of our research, we stumbled on some unexpected findings. For instance, we discovered that the XY relationship you have as an employee with your boss has impacted and will continue to affect your employment, and cloud your judgment, about what your administrators and supervisors need. In a word, XY theory™ explains why so often the person who gets the promotion should be the one who gets the demotion or the pink slip. But we all know that in business, things don't work the way we expect. You will learn more about how personality impacts careers in volume II of XY Theory. You will better understand why, and *what* you can do about it.

Because X and Y personalities approach the workplace differently and with very different skill sets, supervisors would also benefit from being able to match personalities to specific programs and projects for maximum efficiency.

Even political choice is affected by XY personalities, so I have devoted chapters in book two to business and politics.

A Few Questions to Ponder before We Begin

If already in a relationship, answer the following:

- When was the last time your partner told you "I love you," without you asking or saying it first?
- Have you ever asked your partner a question, received no response, and then asked the question again, a little louder, only to be met with a cold, blank stare?
- Does your partner pull his or her hand away when you are trying to be affectionate while walking in public?
- Are you still puzzled as to why your partner thinks it's OK to sit and watch you do all the housework, while never offering to help?
- One client told her story as follows: My husband is so quiet and non-communicative that even with my three small children to care for, I often find myself *"lonely and thirsting for conversation."* Is this your experience too?
- Another woman said she'd been married to the same man for 45 years, but he was so private that most days he seemed like a stranger. Have you ever felt this way?
- On the other hand, do you ever get tired of listening to your partner drone on and on about stories you've heard a thousand times?

- Do you sometimes wish your partner would just give you the CliffsNotes™, or summarize the story, when telling you about his or her day? Have you ever wondered whether your partner feels this way about you?
- Do you sometimes feel that you need some solitude, some alone time away from your talkative or nagging partner, so that you can gather your thoughts?
- If you've been divorced or separated and have kids, does it just break your heart to see the extremes to which your partner will go to avoid seeing his or her own child or to avoid paying child support?

These and other questions will be answered as we explore XY together. I can assure you that the science behind XY theory will change how you view everything and everyone in your life, and I'm happy to be able to take this journey with you.

Chapter 1

How Relationships End Before They Begin

Great Expectations

*D*o you remember the last time you went on a first date? If you're already married, that may have been some time ago. But if you're not currently in a relationship, you probably do remember it. The first date in a relationship is magical. You're full of hope and expectations, giddy with anticipation. In fact, scientists tell us that our bodies release powerful chemicals that add to the magic, the butterflies in the stomach, the feeling of falling in love. I remember the last time I went on a "first date," too. I remember where it was, a lot of what was said, and a little of the clothes we wore. Not bad for a guy, I am told. But I especially remember that my companion for the evening brought cue cards! She was afraid the date might stall, that I might not engage in enough conversation, derailing the relationship train even before it left the station. Oh, and she used every one of those cards, too, asking questions such as, "What's your favorite movie of all time? What's your fondest childhood memory? Do you enjoy walks on the beach or going to a museum or a play?"

I laughed when the cards came out. I'd done a lot of dating but had never been subjected to cue cards before. All the time, I was thinking, "I can carry a conversation just fine, thank you." However, as a psychologist, I understood what Sophie was trying to do. I also knew I could manipulate her by the way I answered her questions, if I really wanted to. I knew, too, that even if I didn't pay attention to what she was saying and answered "yes" to the questions she asked, I would be right more than 80 percent of the time: Yes, I love walks on the beach; yes, I really dig museums and plays; of course, I love children and have every intention of being married one day soon and having a family of my own.

Most people begin a first date by asking "fluff": the obvious, closed-ended questions that any dating representative can answer "yes" to. We all want to believe; we want this one to be *the* one. The "no" questions are saved for later in the relationship or the marriage—either to be asked or discovered, but saved for much later. The goal is to get through this first date without a hitch. So I got through it. In doing so, what I really

20

did was start headfirst into another relationship—one that my own research on compatibility testing would later show had no chance *from the very beginning.*

With a single test, we can now know whether the relationship we're considering will work out, or if the marriage we're already in will ever improve. One woman waited (or wasted) 17 years just to find out what she could have known before going to the altar—that her husband liked who *he* was and never intended to change, even a little.

Just about everyone brings two personalities to the table on the very first date. The second more obscure personality is the predictor of relationship success and compatibility. It is typically either an X or Y type personality, and determines whether couples will be happy or distressed and frustrated with each other. This is the basis of the XY theory that I will share with you in this book.

If you are in an unhappy relationship or a failing marriage, the first thing I want you to do is to quit beating up on yourself emotionally for the choices you've made. As you take this journey with me to discover what XY theory is all about, you'll soon become aware of how many unconscious forces conspired to place you in exactly the relationship you are in today. You didn't *choose* the person you're with by chance (though it might have been a chance meeting). You didn't decide to stick it out and stay with the one you're with because you're a "sucker" for punishment and pain. Strong forces of personality and chemistry pull individuals together and then conspire with their hormones and biology to prevent them from walking away. As a result, the odds of choosing the right man or woman are *not* in your favor. But XY theory, and the latest research you'll learn about in the next few hours, can level the playing field and even give you the edge so that you are more in control of your relational destiny. You will be the one calling the shots, perhaps for the first time. Success in a relationship does not come from giving it extra time or extra effort or by getting more *practice* but rather comes from finding the best match from the start.

Here is the real question: "Is what you saw in those early days of courtship (to use an old term) what you find in the person you're with right now? Is this the type of man or woman you thought you would have? Or were you, like most of us, stunned by who you were dancing with when the happy music stopped—when the frequent calls stopped, when the flowers stopped, when the pampering and the promises stopped. No one likes friends who say to us after the bottom drops out of our lives, "I told you so!" I'll put it another way instead: "I *could* have told you so." No, really, I could have. By the end of this book, you'll be convinced that I could have. More importantly, I'm certain you'll be able to, as well. There are a host of seemingly benign questions you can ask that to the listener would seem non-probing or non-intrusive, but these questions pro-vide a lot more information than your date or mate intended to share with you. But we'll get into that later.

In conducting research for this book, we at The Jacob Research Institute™, were interested in discovering the one factor or ingredient that determines whether partners will ultimately succeed or fail. Basically, most people want to be loved and cherished. Deep down inside, we want to be able to say "I do" to one significant other. This individual will be closer to you than your own parents, your best friends, even your children. If all goes well, you two will become so close that you wouldn't want to be apart. You'll contemplate spending the rest of your lives together, growing in intimacy and love every day. Eventually, someone will propose—in our society, that's becoming increasingly nontraditional: it need not be the man. Regardless of who proposes, the *expectation* is that a bond between two souls will be formed and will continue to grow and strengthen for the rest of their lives. This is the expecta-tion and should be the primary goal of both individuals. The problem arises in how to achieve this and whether couples with different personalities will survive completely differing approaches on what needs to be done to make each other happy for a lifetime.

In this book, I will teach you why the foolish, fluffy ques-tions we typically ask on first dates are only time-fillers, if not time wasters, and how to replace them with questions that will let you know before the end of the first date (at least before the end of this book) whether a new love venture is worth pursuing. Or whether you should fake an allergic reaction after eating the appetizers and run to your car.

If you were asked to rate your current or previous relationship on a scale of 1 to 5, ("1" being unbearable and "5" being excellent), what would your response be? It might surprise you to learn how your partner would rate your relationship. Many of the people we tested at The Jacob Research Institute[1] who said their feelings hovered around "unhappy" or "poor" were shocked to find that their partner answered "good" or "excellent." Yet this shouldn't come as such a surprise; after all, we know that some of us "give" more sacrificially to the relationship than our partners do. Our partners, in turn, will feel more benefitted by being in the relationship and, as a result, will tend to rate it higher.

Other responders at the Research Institute rated their relationship "excellent," but everything they described after that point seemed (to those of us conducting the research) to contradict the rating. So let me ask you directly: Are you truly happy? If you are, this book will teach you steps to fortify the relationship you have and even increase your satisfaction with it. But maybe you've convinced yourself, as so many have, that "tolerable" is good enough. Scientists doing marital research have admitted that the often quoted divorce rate of 40 percent to 50 percent for first marriages is somewhat misleading. This is because the divorce rate for second marriages is quite a bit higher, and a large percentage of those who stick it out with their first or second partner are very unhappy, or resigned to their fate, putting up with the mediocre marriage for the kids or for financial stability.

Just yesterday, a friend called to ask me which I thought was worse: tolerating a poor marriage or being lonely and single. This is quite a personal matter, isn't it? So many factors come into play, such as an individual's sense of morality and level of commitment and the specific circumstances (e.g., whether there is infidelity or abuse). Even as a close friend knowing all the facts, you're almost tempted to flip a coin before answering such a question and may go either way.

But if I asked you that question—having had you take the XY Personality test[2] and knowing the results before raising the question—I could know your true feelings about it with more than 90 percent accuracy, based simply on whether you had an X or Y type personality. It's important to know how your partner would answer that question, too, because the response might give you clues about how she views commitment or how hard he would work to make a marriage work. But I'm getting ahead of myself again.

The Dare

What if someone told you that before you looked for a lover or life partner, they could tell you exactly what your chances were for being loved by this person; whether he would eventually commit to a long-term relationship, be a good father to your children (even if the two of you were separated by circumstance or divorce); whether he would be a good communicator or be the strong, silent type for the rest of your lives; whether he would be loving and affectionate, helpful with chores around the house, or prefer to spend his time alone watching TV, playing X-Box, working, or spending time with his male friends instead of with you? You would probably think your friend was crazy to even suggest she could find a way to give you all these safeguards. It would seem unbelievable that she could tell the end…from the beginning.

Well, my friends tricked me or goaded me into doing just that. They were more tired of my dating life than I was. They laughed at my choice of women. I laughed at the fact that they were bothered by it more than I was. But now I was between relationships, and this was as good a time as any to take them up on their challenge.

"You're the psychologist and you're not in a committed relationship!" one in the group teased. "What do you expect of the rest of us?" OK, that one stung a bit, even though they knew I was choosing instead to focus on the large volume of work we had at the institute. No laughing matter now. Now, I would scour the literature on everything written about relationships in the last 25 years. I would take a look, particularly at what has not worked, and compare that with what I was doing in my own relationships.

My background in psychometrics (science of test measurement) and the college courses I taught for years in applied behavior analysis led me to create one test that would measure two factors, or variables: the two factors that occurred most frequently in difficult relationships. But I felt I still needed to turn the tables on my friends the following day.

Armed with a few details about their lives, I figured it was time for a little payback. I knew that one of them had a boyfriend she couldn't trust. "Marie, I can create a test that can tell you why you can't trust your boyfriend; and Suzie, I can tell you why two of your last three boyfriends cheated and why you always date the same losers; and Jeanne, you've been dating your guy for three years, but no one here has ever met him. He hasn't told you he loves you *yet*, and you know more about the FBI agent who lives in your building than you know about him."

Well, it was on, now. No smiles, no counter attacks. Then one of them mumbled, "Well, bring it," and quickly walked away, and that was that.

If I Knew Then What I Know Now

One of the girls from the teasing squad, Marie, slipped in to see me later in the day. I thought she wanted to apologize for making me the target of their teasing earlier, and I was about to assure her that it was all in good fun and that I wasn't taking anything personally, when she suddenly burst into tears. I quickly closed my office door and offered her a tissue.

"Do you think you could really do it?" she asked between all that sobbing.

"Do what?" I asked.

"Do you think you could create a test to tell whether two people are truly compatible?"

I assured her that I could, that it wouldn't be the first of its kind and that, in fact, I had a head start because I had been thinking about this whole compatibility question for years.

"Well, that is good," she said, looking only slightly consoled. "But promise me that you'll create a test that could predict the outcome without two people even getting involved. Don't focus on marital satisfaction. I think your goal should be to spare couples any pain in the first place." Then she teared up again and turned to leave.

"Wait one minute. Hold on," I said. "Tell me what's wrong."

"I had a fight with my boyfriend over lunch. A stupid, unnecessary argument. We had just finished eating and had been getting along quite well when out of the clear blue, he said to me, "If I knew then (two years ago) what I know now, I would never have asked you out, and we wouldn't be sitting here right now."

"What! He didn't really say that," I said, as she shook her head.

"Yes, he did. I felt like he had punched me in the stomach. I asked him why he would say such a cruel thing. He explained that I was too quiet for him and that he'd been hoping for someone more like his ex-wife. Someone more extroverted, more interesting. He said he should have done his homework and checked me out before he asked me out. John, I was 30 at the time and already feeling a bit desperate. If my bio-logical clock was ticking then, it sure is clanging now, at 33. I wasted three years of my life with that fool. Three years. And we never had one argument. I thought everything was fine. There are enough relationship satisfaction tests out there, I bet. You need a test to help people like me to say no before the first date. That moron said he didn't know why he was attracted to me in the first place, that we should never have gone on that first date."

I explained to Marie that her boyfriend wasn't talking about introversion and extroversion, even though from his choice of words, it seemed like he thought he was. "But I hear what you're saying", I told her. "I'll do what I can." As she slowly walked out of the office, I realized she was right. The relationship regrets many have as they look back are about the wasted years. Any test I created would have to be a pre-test, rather than a post-test that simply shows what went wrong, after the years of someone's life are gone.

The most colorful and accomplished researcher in the literature review was John Gottman, a psychologist who runs a research lab in Seattle and who was previously trained in mathematics at MIT. I liked his scientific and, at times, statistical approach to his research. He exposed a lot of myths about couples in relationships through conducting actual studies on them at his lab in Seattle, Washington[3]. He said that contrary to popular opinion among therapists, poor-quality communication was not always primarily responsible for couples' marital or relational problems. In fact, he said, some couples who had frequent fights found healthy ways to stay together, and not every couple who refused to address their problems fell apart. Yet, communication kept showing up as a primary cause with the couples I tested. If not communication style or even quality, it had to be another aspect of communication that was wreaking havoc in relationships, and I wasn't about to give up until I found out what that was.

Perhaps the revelation from studies done in Gottman's Seattle "Love Lab" that stuck with me the most was the fact that he could predict, after observing a couple interact for only

15 minutes, whether their marriage would fail or succeed. I set out to do the same, but at the beginning of the relationship before anyone got hurt.

There Is Neither Male Nor Female

I know right off the bat that this concept is going to make you feel uncomfortable for a few reasons. The first is that even though we live in a society with a lot of "gender confusion," as well as gender clarification and exposure (from TV shows such as *The Modern Family* or movies like *The Kids Are Alright*), many are still more comfortable with clearly defined roles. So I'll tell you upfront that this section has nothing to do with anyone's sexual preference or orientation; it has everything to do with relationships and how you "relate" to the opposite sex. The second reason this concept might be uncomfortable is that up until now, almost every book written on relationships has pigeon-holed us in neat male and female categories that, frankly, no longer apply when assessing a couple's compatibility. Not every man is from the planet Mars and not every woman is from the planet Venus. If you don't agree, you should stay with me throughout this book as we examine what the latest research shows.

We've worked really hard for almost half a century to get our young girls to see themselves in nontraditional roles, such as the military, engineering, medicine, and law, while our great social experiment has allowed them to model themselves after their mothers with high-powered careers and pushed them to engage in previously male-dominated areas like competitive sports. Meanwhile, we've softened our boys. We've told them it's OK for boys to cry (and it is), and we encouraged them to show their emotional side, their soft side (think *Mr. Mom*). Many boys today see their fathers taking on the role of child care and participating in helping mom with household duties, much more so than in any previous generation. Some have suggested the alternative view, that the role reversals are the unintended product of a rise in single parent homes where the boys lack a male role model and the girls see mom taking on the toughening role of being both mom *and* dad.

Behavioral scientist Sandra Bem contends that masculinity and femininity should comprise "separate personality dimensions."[4] I agree, though as you will see, I have chosen to label those dimensions very differently in my own research. Bem believes that a person who is very masculine by most standards can still possess tenderness, empathy, emotional sensitivity, and other traits stereotypically thought of as feminine, and vice versa. Those who exhibit both stereotypically masculine and feminine traits are described as displaying *psychological androgyny*, which has nothing to do with their sexuality and everything to do with their psychology. Studies further show that psychologically androgynous men are more likely to tolerate their partner's flaws, more likely to adapt or adjust to their differences, and more likely to express tender feelings of love and affection toward their partners. Further, there is evidence that "feminine" traits such as empathy, tenderness and nurturance are predictors of relationship and marital happiness in women as well as men. We will take a closer look at this later in the book.

In fact, today's magazine articles reporting on parenting studies have men almost on par with women in helping out around the home. One study referenced by Bernard Salt in The Australian Newspaper, indicated that the disparity between the amount of domestic housework done by women, compared to men is still vast, with women spending on average 117 minutes on housework compared to 54 minutes for men even during the difficult years of child rearing.[5] Still, the decades-old experiment has worked like a charm. To date, 38 percent of women we've tested have come out with Y type personalities (what would previously have been stereotyped as masculine), with characteristics we've traditionally thought belonged only to men, while 25 percent of men have tested as X types. And even though you're not clear yet what these personality types mean, trust me when I tell you that the results so far show that there is enough crossover to suggest that when it comes to relationships, the portrayal of male vs. female is obsolete. We are all witnesses to this global paradigm shift, though books still portray women as the relationally disadvantaged "species."

The gender that is thought to be disadvantaged is clearly portrayed in the best-selling titles of books on relationships such as these: *Have A New Husband by Friday* (Really? By this Friday?), *The Man Whisperer (Why would women need special training to "tame" their men?),* and *What Women Want Men to Know.*[6]

Try this recent bestseller: *Act Like a Lady, Think Like a Man.*[7] I really must pause here to ask this: As a male author, is it a superior position to think like we do? The last man I interviewed (literally one day before I wrote this) wanted his wife to know that although he was not at all a "wuss" (his words, not mine), he was fully aware that her attempts to show him more affection were just that—mere attempts; that he really enjoyed hugging and cuddling even though he knew that she did not and that he wished she would communicate more.

Here's another title... *Why Men Don't Listen and Why Women Can't Read Maps.*[8] Seriously? Women, are you comfortable with that designation? "Can't read a map?" I personally read maps just fine, but I still get lost. A lot. Am I less of a man?

How about this one: *How to Improve Your Marriage without Talking about It.*[9] Do you want to let your partner off the hook that easily? Not talking because it makes him or her uncomfortable?

Then there is this one, *Becoming the Woman of His Dreams*.[10] (His dreams? Why not *How to Become the Man of Her Dreams*?)

Don't get the wrong impression here. These are all good books that have helped millions tremendously, including me, but perhaps we need more than a book that in effect tells us this about men: "We are different; please just try and understand us." And though I get the metrics of the self-help industry, and I know that women buy and read more self-help books than men, probably by more than a 2 to 1 margin, the implication in the titles betrays the bias in our society. And the bias is this: If there is a problem in the relationship, it is the woman who needs to fix it; she needs to change who she is to make things work. If it doesn't work, it's her fault. She should have tried harder. After all, men are men. Immovable, inflexible, unbending, unyielding. We are, after all, from another planet.

This is not only unfair but inaccurate. One person *rarely* changes the quality of a relationship if the other person is inflexible. And even more surprising, perhaps, is how much our society has changed since we've started asking our women to share our burden in the workforce and carry the double load of full-time provider and full-time homemaker. Luckily not all men are inflexible, unemotional dolts, and quite a few women

I know read maps just fine. (The rest use GPS, just like I do!) And by the way, the title of this section, "There is Neither Male Nor Female" is not new or original. It is 2000 years old, plucked from the writing of the Apostle Paul, straight from the Bible, and we are just now figuring out what an old Jewish preacher already understood so well.

Roy F. Baumeister wrote a book with the catchy title *Is There Anything Good About Men?* [11]

Before we take a look at his work, let me ask you: "Is there anything good about men?" If you are a woman who has suffered enough at the hands of men, you might be tempted to answer this question in the negative. But being the sociologist that Baumeister is, he chose not to answer it directly, nor would it have been his biggest contribution if he had. This was clearly not the most important question the scholar chose to answer in his book.

By far, the most important contribution is his discussion on personalities. Specifically, on gender and personality. Baumeister is one of the many sociologists currently identifying our perspective that most of us have one personality in social settings and yet another in relationships. Where we have run into problems in choosing a partner is when we observe someone at work or play, notice how funny and animated and easygoing that individual is, and assume that this is the person we should take home to mother. But quite often, nothing is further from the truth. And this, in part, is the reason so many women complain that at home their husbands behave nothing like they do in public. These thousands of women (and sometimes men) were the hopeful captors of attractive butterflies who were captured and caught on a moonlit night and taken home, where after sometime, they eventually folded their wings in silence and became brooding and "moth-like" in appearance and behavior. When you ask someone to describe on an Internet dating site who they really are, what you get is who they are *socially*. Almost no one talks about who they are *relationally*.

I have never read a profile that said, "I am the life of every party. But take me home and watch me wither like spinach in a Crockpot. I might be talking up a storm now, but when I'm alone with you at home—once I know everything about you there is to know and I don't feel the need to impress you anymore—I'll have nothing to say."

Or try this: "At the last staff party, even though you noticed me working the room like a tap dancer, the moment you take me with you and we decide to be together, I'll tell you right now, *I am going to need my space*. But you have to figure this out on your own because I'm not much of a talker in relationships, and I would prefer that you painstakingly figure all this out as you go along. There will be times that you'll ask me questions and I will not answer you. Please don't feel the need to repeat those questions or try to say them louder. I heard you the first time. I just wanted to be sure that what you were asking is a rhetorical question, and not one that really requires an answer. I've noticed that sometimes you just like to chit-chat, with no real function or purpose in mind, and that's OK. Because it only takes me a minute to figure out that we're not talking about anything I am interested in, so I can just tune you out."

Or this: "Here's one more thing. Remember on the day of our wedding when I said, 'I do?' Well, I did! I said 'for better or for worse,' too. That pretty much covered everything, didn't it? Well, I meant it—the whole 'I love you' thing. But I did not expect to have to repeat it every day for the rest of your life just because you're insecure and lack that self-assurance. If I'm still here, I'm probably still in love with you. You can tell me you love me as much as you like, but please don't make me uncomfortable by expecting or forcing me to reciprocate."

And on and on and on. When it comes right down to it, the thing that matters the most to the success of your relationship is the relationship personality that partners bring to it at the start. In this book I will argue that these personalities are, for the most part, non-negotiable, and you're better off knowing what you've got. Therefore, you need to be taught how to make that determination very early in a friendship or relationship to avoid making a mistake down the road.

Most of us have one of two basic personalities we can bring to the table, X or Y (and two other combinations that we'll learn about later). The majority of unhappy couples are XY combinations. Most of the problems you hope to avoid as you sit opposite your date or your husband or girlfriend, trying to read his or her mind to determine the motives behind the confusing actions, are caused by XY personality differences. Your last friendship, your last relationship, your last marriage, probably ended because of it. Gnawing questions like: Is he playing me? Does she really like me? Does he have commitment issues? Will this date end in marriage, or will he keep putting stuff off? If we did get married, would it last?

These can all be answered before the end of the first date. In fact, many people who have read excerpts of this book and gave the XY Personality test to their date, or were told the basic concept of XY theory before the book's publication, never bothered to go on the second date! XY theory is real and dangerous for those who don't have honest intentions and would prefer to keep true motives hidden. On the other hand, it can save you years of trying to change the wrong man or trying to capture the heart of the uninterested woman because personalities tend to be quite constant over time.

The XY Personality test will also analyze the strength of your current relationship or marriage and warn you of potential problems down the road. Certain personality types are more susceptible to many of the factors that threaten marriages and more prone to power struggles, control issues, conflict resolution problems, emotional infidelity, and a traditional way of thinking that leads to unfair imbalances of domestic chores and child care. Whether the probability is high for these to happen to you can be known before the end of the first date.

Dr. Gottman, the godfather and guru of marital research referenced earlier in the chapter—who could tell close to the end of the relationship whether it would succeed or imminently fail—used observed communication between the couple as well as body language to make his determinations. Yet when he proposed that communication per se was not as critical to the success of a relationship as many had thought, because many couples who didn't communicate that much had relationships that weren't derailed by conflict, I believe he was on the cusp of highlighting an important facet of XY theory. The point is that communication isn't necessarily just about conversation, and if both partners in a relationship are low communicators (which would mean they're both less inclined to rely on communication to solve problems), then lack of communication is not likely to be a source of problems for either partner. Gottman found that an escalation in negative communication, which deteriorates into criticism and finally contempt, was more destructive to the satisfaction of the couple.[12]

X and Y personality types refer not just to communication styles but to how each uses communication to deal with much of the heavy lifting that relationships require. You're an X communicator if tests determine that your responses to XY test questions show not only a preference for using conversation to communicate goals, dreams, experiences, and problems, but a *need* and desire for your partner to do the same (at least more than 50 percent of the time). Those who are less likely to use or need conversation to meet the requirements of a relationship are Y communicators. What Dr. Gottman discovered when his research found a class of couples who were not hampered by the destabilizing nature of conflict, showing relationship outcomes less influenced by communication, was probably, YY couples: individuals who neither used nor saw communication as a basic need for their relationship's survival.

By the time we're finished, you'll know exactly what these letter combinations mean and what they tell about your relationship personality. More importantly, you'll know exactly who to go out with and who to avoid, or what to do to improve the situation you're already in. There's much to share, too. Like answers to these questions: Will he ever cheat? Why won't he help with the housework? Would he make a good parent? Will he get along with the in-laws? Can he hold a job? Will he be successful at it?

Or other personal questions: Why does my boyfriend ignore me when I talk to him? Why would my husband prefer to watch sports or hang out with his buddies on a golf course all day than spend time with me? Why won't he help me with the kids? Why does my wife seem so emotionally cold at times? Is there anything I can do about it?

You will learn that the answers to these questions are *already* stored in your partner's DNA, ready to be downloaded and deciphered if you have the right tools. And once discoveries are made, you'll find that how your relationship ends is most often decided *before* it even begins. So let's take a closer look at this theory, shall we?

Chapter 2

Dangerous Need

W hat we consistently found in our research, at the Jacob Research Institute, was predictable unhappiness, distress, and a drop in relationship satisfaction for the X type person who was saddled in an XY relationship. But, also for the less disclosing Y who did not feel free to share much, but chose rather to maintain his or her aura of strength and infallibility. We live in an age and time when independence is praised, and dependence on others is shunned and discouraged. One woman who came in to see us with her two boys, already in their twenties, explained how one of them (the older boy) could turn in to his room on a Friday night, never come out for anything but food (the most basic of needs), and never talk to anyone, not answering his phone or communicating with anyone, until he went off to work on Monday. His brother was the opposite. He needed to talk and relate and socialize as well as spend a few hours per day on the weekend talking to his girlfriend on the phone, if they could not meet in person.

This mother seemed to despise the talkative, friendlier boy as she went on to explain how much he was like his father, while the non-communicator was more like she was. She chided the talker, not for being so talkative but for being so "needy." She ended her tirade by saying, "My younger son should be more like me. I don't need people!"

She is not alone. This kind of thinking has seeped into our consciousness, particularly in Western nations. It's not uncommon to hear a group of friends say to a close friend after a breakup, "Why don't you spend some time alone? Like six months, or so. Maybe even a year. You shouldn't *need* to always *be with* someone. You should take a break to kind of find yourself." And this thinking has taken some root. The next time you're in between relationships, try telling someone close to you that you plan on getting back in the saddle immediately, and see what they say. Please don't misunderstand what I'm getting at here. I do believe there is a need to take some time off to regroup before jumping right back into another relationship. We're aware that *sometimes,* unhealthy individuals get their self-esteem from being in a relationship, but this isn't always the case.

The fact is that Y type individuals are often in less of a hurry to get back into a committed relationship than X types.

Conversely, X types are more anxious to do so because of the psychological benefits they derive from it, along with the need to "relate," to communicate, and to bond with another human being. The "need to need" and be needed is built into the DNA and personality of an X type. It predisposes and constantly pushes them to take the necessary steps to satisfy this need, the easiest way being to find someone to "relate" to, or get into a relationship with, and they accomplish this initially, through communication.

I didn't have an opportunity to test this lady's two boys, but she tested Y type, and I am betting that her boys split their personalities between X and Y. If you are an X type individual, you too will find that you *need* people to relate to, but you don't need to depend on them in a psychologically unhealthy way. We've also found from our research that it's not enough to simply go out there (if you're between relationships) and find an X type if you're an X, or a Y type if you're a Y type individual. In fact, it's downright dangerous to go out and simply hook up with another X because you *are* one—you might still find that you "need" this individual more than this person "needs" you.

Our research showed that when it comes to "communicative need," there are various levels of need. So it isn't enough to say that you are an X communicator. You and your partner need to have about the *same level* of need. We found that couples who were more than one level apart experienced discomfort, dissonance, and distress, very similar to the mixed couples in XY relationships whose communicative mismatch creates a strain.

Psychiatrist Louann Brizendine found from her research that there are hormones produced in the brain that make us want to bond, love, and connect with others.[13] The effect of these hormones and chemicals, she purports, is the reason teenage girls, for instance, are always on the phone—because they actually *need* to communicate to produce these hormones that reduce their stress levels. I have devoted chapter 12 to our discussion on the role chemicals play on our various needs.

Let us turn our attention now to the various levels of need that exist in the XY theory model.

100	_____	Extremely High Need
X	_____	High Need
X	_____	Moderate Need
50	_____	Borderline Need
Y	_____	Low Need
Y	_____	Extremely Low Need

The full version of the XY Personality test measures need on a scale from 1 through 100. But at this point, it is important to note that the best matches occur if you test at the same level of need as your partner. If he, as an X, had a moderate need for conversation, you would have the best match communicatively if you did, too. If your need was moderate and his was borderline (see the diagram above), you would still have a relationship that could easily be workable with some adjustments because he would be only one level away. Often this is tolerable, if not sometimes desirable.

We've seen couples in which one partner's communication scores were as high as 95 (extremely high need) and the other partner's score as low as 15 (extremely low need). To my knowledge, after coming for testing at the Jacob Research Institute and following our program for XY couples, they're still together today. But such a vast spread between levels of need is not ideal.

In general, clients' number scores on the XY Personality tests will not be presented at this stage because I believe it's infinitely more useful for people in relationships—or interested in relationships—to have "type awareness" in which they're aware of their basic personality type (X or Y) first. After that, knowledge of one's *level* of need is next in importance, as this level drives behavior, expectations, and satisfaction in relationships.

Dating Deliberately

Most of us will admit that when it comes to dating, we are with whom we're with because of a chance meeting. "I saw her on the job. She looked good. So I started a conversation with her and she seemed nice, so I asked her out."

"I noticed him in the aisle walking ahead of me at the store. He was tall and good-looking. He looked a little lost. There's just something about a man buying his own food in a grocery store by himself that I find a bit sexy. I went up to him to ask if I could help him find something, and instead he asked me out for coffee. He didn't have a ring on his finger, and frankly, that was good enough for me. The rest, as they say, is history."

"Frank and I met at a bar, and we shouldn't have. I know what they say. You won't find Mr. Right at any of the *wrong* places. But I'm 31, a single mom, and I work out of my home. If I don't go to a pub or a nightclub to meet someone, where would I meet them? I'd like to settle down and have one more child, but my biological clock is ticking. Pretty loudly. I'm surprised you can't hear it!"

These were three examples on how typical chance meetings occur. They're all plausible, but they're only scenarios. This one I'm about to share with you is not.

Katherine was an associate professor at a small college in a large city. She was attractive, in her mid-twenties, and obviously intelligent and career-minded. But her intelligence didn't show in her choices for a companion. Katherine was tired of dating men with little ambition and lots of commitment issues. So when the young man approached her and invited her to his favorite church instead of his favorite club, she felt that her fortunes had changed. His height, physique, and good looks didn't hurt this man's chances with her either. He took her to his church, where she observed him at close range.

He had a child, a four-year-old boy—who was dressed in a dashing suit—and he treated him like a prince. He clearly was a good father, and that impressed her quite a bit. Therefore, 10 months later, she joined his church. One day she discovered that one moment of indiscretion between them led to an unplanned pregnancy. But she wasn't worried. She was confident that the man who had repeatedly professed his love for God, and his adoration of her, would do the right thing. He would ask to marry her long before her mistake would show.

Katherine set up a meeting with their minister and her boyfriend. They talked about their predicament, and the minister agreed to perform a quiet ceremony. She breathed a sigh of relief. She'd felt certain that her minister would throw the book at them and condemn this careless couple to the fires of hell. But he didn't. He was as forgiving as he was caring. He prayed with them and asked them to make their decision quickly, letting him know as soon as possible when they would need his services so that a date could be reserved.

They went back to her apartment. She excitedly sat on the sofa. He sat opposite her, pensive and nervous. He explained that he was in no way prepared to get married at this time, so she would have to deal with the repercussions of carrying a baby to term and birthing her child out of wedlock in a fairly conservative church. He felt this was the best time to inform her (for the first time) that he had *four* other children, all boys, with other women. He promised to take care of the child because, as she could tell, "he loves children." But he had made a decision years ago to remain single—at least unmarried, because he didn't believe in marriage.

She began to sob.

So where did Kathy go wrong? It's easy to blame the outcome on any number of shortcomings. Was it an error of judgment? She took a chance on his morality, and the outcome was sad and unfortunate. But was this extreme example of a commitment issue, in any way predictable?

Dating (and Mating) Errors of Judgment

Ninety-seven percent of all mammals have commitment issues—97 percent! OK, let me state that exactly as I got it from the researchers. Ninety-seven percent of all mammals are polygamous. They get together for mating and mating alone. Some stick around to help the lucky female, but most do not. The females raise their pups alone, no matter how large the litters might be. As do many human beings, the females generally look strictly at superficial variables such as height, size, strength, color, and appearance when picking who will father the children. There is no error of judgment here because for this 97 percent, what they see is what they get.

Some would say that as the highest order of mammals, we continue in that vein—even as the *thinking* species—to choose our partners according to what today might be seen as superficial. Furthermore, the younger we are as adults, the *less* pre-thought and deliberation is likely to go into our choices.

Psychologist Abraham Maslow listed food, shelter, etc, and then "safety" and "security" as some of the basic lower-level needs of humans.[14] In lower-order animals, safety would be related to size, appearance, and brawn—a male's ability to protect the female. As humans (and perhaps unlike animals such as chimpanzees or coyotes, where males look mostly alike) we have added good looks to the equation too. Some scientists believe the further removed a woman is from her teenaged years, the more important security or a man's ability to *provide* for her and a family becomes. This pushes safety concerns (in developed societies) and other variables to second or third place. But research shows that this all changes after middle age, until companionship becomes the primary concern in later years. The "bad boy" syndrome (where women feel they're more attracted to "bad boys" with their rugged good looks, couldn't-care-less attitudes, and sex appeal) certainly decreases with age. Even at its peak, psychologists contend that these women are looking for what some call "coconuts": alpha males who look tough and hard on the outside but are soft and sensitive on the inside. Naturally, this can be a source for errors in judgment because—sticking to the metaphor—it's almost impossible to know what's inside a coconut until you've bought it and cracked it open.

But we still have not solved Katherine's dilemma. How did she get caught like that? An educated, beautiful, accomplished, professional woman who had no baggage until this loser saddled her with some. Yes, the lucky lady had twins!

Parallax Errors in Relationships

In physics, parallax errors are committed when readings are taken, such as when gauges, or the level of liquid in a measuring cup or cylinder are read.[15] The point is that there is the actual reading, and there is the approximate or perceived reading from the observer's point of view or point of reference; these vary relative to the angle the reading is being taken from. This is most easily demonstrated using a large clock or the watch on your wrist. Observing from different angles, the exact time changes relative to the angle from which the hour hand or minute hand in particular, is viewed.

A type of parallax error occurs in relationships as well; one person perceives or attributes certain personality traits to the person he or she is interested in when considered from a certain angle, or view. Though many types of errors abound, in this chapter we will talk about one type of parallax error that Katherine made when choosing a mate.

Moral Parallax Error

I chose this type because Moral Parallax Error addresses Kathy's specific problem and helps us to understand a little of how parallax works.

Kathy altered her perception of her church guy when she made the unconscious decision to view him only through religious eyes rather than approaching the experience cautiously, as she normally would. She made the assumption that because he claimed to be religious, he was also spiritual. An easy mistake to make. This young man wouldn't even hold her hand in the beginning and so avoided any sexual exchange for the first six months. He seemed serious and trustworthy—not the type of man with the character that would permit him to do what he did. Why would anyone wait six months to touch a woman unless he was really into her, or, serious about his faith? Well, for him, it was neither. And Kathy made her mistake because of a parallax error—an error of judgment set up by the lens through which Kathy chose to judge her love interest.

I asked her to complete an XY Personality test for herself and to also do one for him. I will cover the tests in greater detail in chapter 11. So that you understand fully what happened to Kathy, I can tell you now that Kathy was able to complete a version of the test known as the XY Perception Test for Reluctant Partners™—created because so many Y types refuse testing. This version of the test done by proxy is 95 percent accurate and gives a true reading of a partner's personality without his or her direct input. A brief version of that test is provided in chapter 11 as well. Naturally, you would need to know your partner for some time to be able to complete the test accurately. Just as I guessed, Kathy was an X type and her boyfriend was a classic Y type, and an extremely low Y, at that—the type that is typically a commitment-phobe and very unlikely to propose to the girl he's currently dating. What was even more problematic for this X type woman was the fact that he would have felt that she was too clingy, too needy, and too nagging. To him, this would have the appearance of a "dangerous" need if not neediness, the destroyer of any prospect of a meaningful or lasting relationship with a Y partner. If he were ever to choose someone, she would not be the one. Not even after they had a second and third child together.

She couldn't know all this before, of course, when she saw him across the street of that bustling city on that fateful day. But she wouldn't have had to. After all, that's what personality tests are for.

What Will You Do When You Get to the Scheideweg?

We've come to what's so dangerous about being in a relationship in which the XY effect, where XY couples begin to experience discomfort, is in full effect. The majority of couples we researched indicated that their XY relationships ended more abruptly than others, and often without warning. One day you're in a happy relationship, the very next, you're being told it's over—that is, if you didn't receive the sudden news by text or email. There are distinct reasons for this and we will cover them several times in this book.

I tried to convey this danger to a German couple I tested. I asked them if they understood what needed to be done whenever they encountered a serious problem in their relationship and found themselves at a fork in the road. This question took us away from our topic because the girlfriend, Gabriele, felt I shouldn't use the phrase, "the fork in the road."

She said, "I'm not familiar with that phrase, 'the fork in the road'. Why would you call it a fork? It has three or four prongs. People don't have three or four choices if they're in a serious relational crisis. They have two choices. Do we stay together or do we go our separate ways, right here, right now."

She continued, "In Germany, we call it the Scheideweg. It's translated 'the split in the road.' It's a split, not a fork."

"You feel that you have only two outcomes because you're in an XY relationship," I told her. But her characterization was correct for her situation and would also describe you, if you too, are in an XY relationship.

At some point in the relationship, you will get to a place in the road where communication fails and conflict resolution skills will be needed to get past that point. But as we'll see in volume II of XY Theory, conflict resolution is a difficult proposition for XY couples, so as an X, you might decide you no longer wanted to wait or, you'll keep hoping that your partner will acknowledge your communication needs, and possibly make a verbal commitment to supply that need. Even in relationships, supply-side economics is often at work and has two sides: the ones whose resources of time and communication are in demand, and who have what their partners need. While on the other side are the partners who are demanding that their needs be met. The demanding X type is often the one to pull the plug on the relationship, tired of the sense of personal devaluation and self-loathing that often befalls the "needier" X type. Failure to find a way to navigate these mine fields in the road often ends the journey. So let me ask you: What will you do when you get to the dangerous "fork in the road"? Will it be for you a small detour? Or the end of the road—the final "scheideweg"?

The Elephant in the Room

Of all modern theorists whose ideas I examined, no one has come closer to inadvertently identifying the key to marital satisfaction or relationship success than Susan Cain in her work on introversion and shyness. As with so many other theorists, she did not point to introversion as providing a key to solving the relationship puzzle, nor should she. After all, this was not the thrust of her book, *Quiet*.[16] But I couldn't help being drawn to the title while writing this book.

When you're writing a book with a premise that the primary difficulty, if not difference, between happy couples and incompatible partners is a difference in communication needs, a book titled *Quiet* grabs you by the throat. Her stories about two characters, Emily and Greg, a husband and wife, tiptoed around the edges of XY theory. According to her thesis, introverts tend to be drawn to extroverts and often make good mates, except when they don't.

She inferred that introverts could at times feel they're experiencing irreconcilable differences with their extrovert partners, whom they are generally drawn to. But one vivid point she made came from her character, Emily, whose feeling was that at social events, people don't go to "relate" but rather to "socialize." This is an excellent distinction and mirrors what we've been discussing about the difference between relationship personality and social personality. But more on Susan Cain's insightful work, later in this book. For now, I'd like to point out that Susan succeeded in walking around the room and identifying more of the XY "elephant in the room" than others have before her.

We do not examine extroversion vs. introversion in this volume of XY theory because X and Y types can be either extrovert or introvert in the public arena. Instead, we identify two other factors that our research indicates play a larger part in relationship dissatisfaction. Dr. Gottman may have found that conversational style wasn't a primary cause of marital failure, but I believe that the reason he could not acknowledge the "elephant" is that research over many decades predisposed us to look at *how* our partner's communication differed from ours, instead of *how much* they communicated.

Cain, to her credit, identified in her book what she called a "communication gap," but applied her accurate observation to extroverts and introverts only, as she should have—to be true to the focus of her book.

There is a communication gap between individuals, a difference in how much each partner communicates. Unfortunately, this difference in total word count (and we have attempted to count the words spoken) is not as obvious as, say, the difference between long hair or short, blue eyes or brown, or a preference for coffee or tea.

Nevertheless, the *difference* in words exchanged— between a Y-type man who talks a little and an X-type woman who talks a lot—causes long-term discomfort and distress. In order for this disparity to occur, someone has to talk more than the other and someone has to talk less. What this means is that at times, the big talker, or X type personality, will ask a question that is heard but not answered—probably *mistaken* for a rhetorical question that the questioner, never wanted or needed answered anyway. It will also mean that the X type person will want to talk about his or her day and will go to elaborate lengths to share with the partner details that he or she doesn't want to hear, has no interest in, and would find boring, if not downright annoying.

Xs are believed to out-communicate Ys by as much as 3 to 1, but this is purely in relationship terms. To accomplish this, the talker will have to start early and finish late. One client complained that her husband talks her ear off from the time they wake up at 4:00 a.m. to get ready for work, a full two hours before she's had her cup of eye-opening espresso. The X type talker also tends to talk about a few topics or some people that her partner would label as gossip.

The Y partner's reaction to verbal overload is escapist in nature and takes many forms. The Y type will ignore, walk away, preoccupy himself or herself with other activities or (especially men) avoid coming home early altogether, arrange 18 holes of golf or a weekend-long fishing trip.

The difference in *how much* an X type talks, compared to her Y partner, her adjustments to deal with the shortage, and his maneuvers to escape from the overload, are not just a difference in personality or disposition.

It is perceived by the X as:

- A slight
- An insult
- A rejection
- A hurt

Most of all, the Y type's way of communicating, tells his partner that he is just not that into his X type mate. Even if he once cared enough about her to go to the altar and say "I do," his silence now pushes her away, causing pain, emotional disconnection, and a breakdown in the intimacy and bonding between the two.

I understand that it will take some effort on my part to convince you that the majority of woes you have ever had in any of your relationships can be traced back to a perceived difference in how much you communicated or how much you wanted to be communicated to—that the bad feelings this difference caused when it first started were like a drop of acid persistently released on a thin sheet of metal until it bore a large hole right through what you thought was solid as steel.

It will also take effort to convince you that complaints of various kinds exchanged between you and your partner were used only to mask the communication problem. But this is the hypothesis I am prepared to argue in this book. We have lots of evidence and research to support this theory, so perhaps the problem is that your partner just couldn't articulate it. Just think how petty it would seem, and immature, to tell a boyfriend or wife that you were packing your things to get out of the house—the relationship and the commitment—because you just couldn't stand one more hour of the silence! Or if you're a Y, not one more pointless conversation.

If you cited infidelity as the cause for leaving? Acceptable. Physical abuse? Sure. If you live in California: irreconcilable differences? Certainly. People grow apart all the time, we understand. It happens. But when was the last time someone told you that he left his wife because she talked too much? Have you ever heard anyone admit that he packed up his stuff and left the love of his life because she was too quiet? Yet once we helped couples analyze the real root of the problem, it came right down to this big "elephant in the room" at least 50 percent of the time. The elephant was missed because though many couples noticed it, they thought the elephant was a small one. A baby. Nothing that should cause too much disruption. But if you've ever seen a baby elephant at close range, you would know it's still big enough to cause severe damage in a tiny room.

And what about the other 50 percent? That turned out to be problems with intimacy. But, you'll have to wait until chapters 4 through 8, where we cover the whole concept in closer detail. You can start today though, to be conscious of the difference between *how much* you communicate, compared to your partner, and whether either of you has ever so much as hinted that there might be an elephant in the room.

Chapter 3

The X Type Personality

Love and Other Stipulations

"*L*aura, I will take you back if you agree not to touch me anymore. Don't hug me, don't kiss me, don't try to hold my hand, and don't expect to hear from me every day. I do not like to communicate as much as you do, so please, keep the conversations short. I get irritated easily, and we don't want to see what that's like again, do we? Stop calling me at work, too. When we have to drive into the city to help my mother once a week, you tend to yap a lot."

Laura didn't answer so her boyfriend continued, "Since we're putting it all on the table, I have to tell you, it annoys me. I like to drive in silence, focus on my driving. You feel the need to make me your shrink. What you need is to get over that neediness." He paused to let it all sink in and then said, "Can you live with these stipulations?"

She said yes softly, and with some resignation reached over to hug and kiss her man. She needed to confirm their reconciliation after being broken up for three months over those very stipulations. But as she touched his shoulder, he snapped immediately, "Were you listening to anything I just said? I don't like you touching me!" Then he mumbled something else and pulled away from her.

What Laura was being required to endure by her boyfriend was unconscionable, but these exchanges occur between men and women only too often. This incident occurred at the end of an 11-month relationship that had been rocky for the two people involved but unbearable to watch from the sidelines. Laura and I had spoken about XY relationships briefly. She understood that her boyfriend, Joel, had a Y type personality, while she had an X type and vowed to give the relationship everything she had. But she could not change his personality any more than she could change her own traits and needs.

She called me immediately after meeting with her beau to tell me what he said. I asked her if she could live up to his requirements. She said that as he spoke, she felt as if he had reached over and strangled her with his remarks, preventing her from presenting her own views, but believed she had no choice but to comply, because she really loved him and intended to keep him at all costs. She was not allowed to call him during the day anymore. She would try her best not to touch him, hold his hand, kiss him, or hug him, just as he had asked. *Some relationship*, she thought.

I felt bad for Laura. I wondered what she actually was allowed to do to show her partner her true feelings. If she were my sister or daughter, I would want to confront him. He didn't suffer from a personality disorder or Asperger's or Tourette's Syndrome, or he might have had an excuse for his rude remarks. This was simply who he was, who he would be every day of his life, as long as he dated a woman with communication and intimacy needs as high as Laura's. He was despicable. Not for having the personality he had, but for the way he manipulated Laura to change hers...and for pushing her or expecting her to alter the core of who she was to satisfy his needs.

Personality Types

There are four personality types identified in more detail in chapter 10. There is the classic X type personality with high scores in communication and high scores on the intimacy scale. The correct designation, then, for classic X types, would be XX. The second personality type is the XY personality. This individual has high communication needs and scores high on the communication scale, while at the same time having low emotional needs, with a score placing him or her on the Y side of the intimacy scale. The third personality type is the YX personality. In a relationship, this individual is not likely to be very communicative and, as a result, is not likely to require much casual conversation from a partner either, except to share intimate feelings. Several authors of self-help books refer to this principle as the "principle of reciprocation." It simply says that people tend to give what they hope to get, but when it comes to mixed relationships such as XY and YX relationships, it's a little more complex than that.

It's not just about *not giving* something that you're not getting; rather, it's about someone not wanting it, not enjoying it, and most times being quite irritated by it. But with the letter X in the secondary position, the indication for the YX individual is that despite not wanting conversation, this partner wants, needs, and is willing to give affection, attention, and emotional support and will use verbal expression to convey care and love. The final personality type is the classic Y type personality. As with the classic X type personality, pure Y types are literally YY types. This means they have a very low need for communication and an equally low need for emotional expression and validation.

In this chapter, we are dealing exclusively with the classic X type personality. If you have purchased this book and are reading this chapter, you are probably X type, having once dated or being now married to a Y type personality. You had no idea what you were getting into. In fact, it seemed like quite a good idea at the start. She seemed like anyone else. He seemed like the man of your dreams. You received a fair share of attention and quite a bit of affection—not only were you allowed to talk as much as you wanted, but he seemed to hang on to your every word.

If you were as unlucky as Brittany, one of our clients, your date wined and dined you, romanced you, and swept you off your feet so fast that you were standing at the altar or chose to move in with this man in less than a year. At some point, though, things changed, even if you never quite made it to the altar. He stopped laughing at your jokes, seemed as though he could not wait for you to end your sentences, let alone your conversations, and you found yourself waiting by the phone a lot, for his calls. You would send him four lines of text message, and if you were lucky, you got back one word, maybe just the letter "K" for OK. But you need to know that you're not alone. There are millions like you enduring the same fate. To date, about 62 percent of women who took the XY test in chapter 11 experienced exactly what you have, and about 25 to 30 percent of men have as well.

When It Comes to X Type Bonding: Communication Is King

Unlike their Y type partners, X types bond by talking and touching. But when it comes to bonding, communication is key. The more Xs communicate, the closer the relationship and the tighter the bond. The XY personality scale is divided into two dimensions, as we'll see in greater detail in chapter 11. The first is the communication scale or, more specifically, the communication needs scale. The second is the secondary needs scale, which measures needs such as attention, affection, and other needs that contribute to a feeling of closeness to one's partner. Therefore, the XX personality types require communication with their partners and have certain emotional needs. The relationship suffers when either of these is not met, and the X type individual feels less than fulfilled in the relationship.

How X Types Communicate

Everything is different about the way X type people communicate, as are their communication needs and expectations compared to Ys. X types communicate in swirls, where they leave one topic half discussed, jump to another topic, and swirl back around again to complete the first. Whereas

Y types communicate in discrete snatches, sound bites, and only on topics deemed functional or centered around their own self-interests. This presents a constant source of conflict between XY couples whenever they try to have casual conversations. X types, aware of their ability to carry on multiple conversations at the same time and often with a group of friends, view it as just another form of multitasking. Barbara De Angeles, the well-known relationship expert, refers to this skill as multi-tracking and sees it as a skill of women. However, our research showed that men who tested as having X type personalities were just as skilled as their female counterparts in multi-tracking. Meanwhile, Y types are unable to keep up with the simultaneous conversations of X types.

As we covered earlier, according to XY theory, we categorize individuals in terms of X and Y type personalities rather than by gender. There are men who have high communication needs, while the women they're with do not. Similarly, there are men with high intimacy needs, while their partners do not have such high needs. In chapter 1, we pointed out that relational personality traits no longer fall along gender lines. So the simultaneous talk and conversational multitasking (or multi-tracking) builds bonds of friendship and relationship, and it demonstrates care and interest for both X type men and X type women. Keep in mind that multi-tracked conversational flow, which Y type men and women struggle to keep up with, not only is difficult for them to understand but also prevents Ys from successfully navigating a conversation with Xs. They're likely to retreat from conversations when their conversational circuits are overloaded.

Y types also have considerable difficulty jumping in and out of any discussion with Xs, particularly when conversations are of little interest to them. Ys are more used to having conversations with those who take turns and talk one at a time, rather than simultaneously, as Xs tend to do. Xs experience a rush as ideas flow from their minds to their mouths, unfettered. In X "speak," this "X burst," or rush, when it continues for some time, is referred to as the X Effect and is a powerful means of bonding that occurs among Xs on a fairly regular basis. It does not require topics of high interest and can occur among friends who see each other every day. A few Ys we interviewed boasted of having experienced at least the individual burst on occasion. For them, this occurred only with good friends they hadn't seen for years and produced a rush that lasted for no more than the few minutes it took for the novelty of renewed friendship to wear off.

If you ever have the opportunity to sit down and listen to three X type individuals, men or women, as they carry on a conversation, you could feel the energy in the interaction: the X Effect at work. You could hear multiple conversations going on at once, sometimes emanating from one speaker. You could tell that three people could carry on five topics at any one time. No one would be confused and no one would be put off or made angry by it. This is how X type communicators communicate, and it is very frustrating to Y types. But it's also the reason many Y type husbands and Y type wives do not want to listen to their significant other for extended periods. And it is why Y type males often make significant attempts to shut down their wives as they try to explain their positions on various topics.

It is not difficult to see why so many Y type partners in large families of talkers are pushed into needing solitude and quiet or alone time or space—because they are overwhelmed by the X bursts and the X flow. The loud outbursts and the continuous flow of chatter. Even having to speak at a volume that is above the decibel level of Xs in excited conversation is off-putting. Very often, a group of X types become so excited with what they're sharing that they quickly fall into this continuous (and to Y types, nauseating) but exuberant "flow."

Barbara and Allan Pease are authors of the book *Why Men Don't Listen and Women Can't Read Maps*.[17] In their book, they point out that the multi-tracking ability allows (X) men and women to not only speak simultaneously but also to listen simultaneously, and to do so on several unrelated topics. But according to the Peases, the effect can't really be seen in younger boys at school, who come home and have no desire to share anything about their school day with their mother. According to the authors, this is because boys and girls have different requirements when it comes to communication. Girls require more communication than boys, so they are happy to share their details up front without being enticed to do so. Parents were told that once boys have used up their allotted resource of words in an effort to talk to the teachers at school, which is a requirement, they shut down and have little to say once they arrive home, where talking isn't mandatory. Translation? According to XY theory, this could be true of either boys or girls, depending on whether they were X type or Y type.

Several hundred X type and Y type men and women were surveyed and interviewed in several states. The general sentiment of X type women was that Y type men would often come home to their families and have nothing to say. When questioned, these individuals admitted to having the same disposition as the children referred to by Barbara and Allen Pease, only not along gender lines. I am convinced that because of the old paradigms, which give rise to the same gender classifications that told us that boys shouldn't cry and girls should learn to cook, the Peases failed to examine their data differently. A more cautious examination would have revealed that not all boys or all girls follow any stereotypical expectation. The other 25 to 40 percent who do not would have raised enough of an uncertainty to alert them and others that a new paradigm was emerging across the world. I should hasten to point out that I have no intention of laying a charge of sloppiness at the feet of other psychologists or scientists. At one time, men and women behaved more predictably, more stereotypically. But that time slipped away quietly and more rapidly in the past two decades.

This paradigm shift was particularly well highlighted in the case of a couple who worked together. Their story was enlightening because the X type husband sat in the same lunchroom as his Y type wife, but they never sat together. According to his report, he would sit there day after day and hear her cracking jokes with her colleagues and coworkers. In fact, wherever she sat in the large lunchroom, people would seek her out because wherever she was, became the "Comedy Corner" at the worksite. She was a social butterfly and the life of the party at lunch, so he couldn't understand why, when she got home, she had nothing left for her own family. He said he could deal with living in silence and being ignored by her, but he could not stand to see the children neglected emotionally.

He felt he had to confront her one night, and this was her response. "You have no idea how difficult it is for me to keep up that act at work. That's not me. I feel I have to do that to fit in, to belong, to be part of the team. I don't think I could ever get a promotion by myself, on my own merits at this job.

You know how I am, quiet and boring. Do you think those traits would get me anywhere? So, I am sorry that you have a problem with the fact that I do what I do to help you keep bread on this family's table. But yes, you're right. When I get home, I feel spent. I really feel like I've used all the words that I have at work, and I don't feel that I want to be bothered when I get home. I just want to feed the kids, sit in front of the TV, and be quiet, and not be nagged all night about it."

While we're on this topic, let's talk about the number of words that X types use during the day, compared to their Y type partners. Several studies, including one from Dr. Brizendine, the author of the book, *The Female Brain*, report a difference between the number of words that men and women used during their day.[18] We talked about the Peases earlier. They suggest that women use 6,000 to 8,000 words per day, including signs and nonverbal signals. Total bits of communication could be in the vicinity of 20,000 units. Conversely, men use 2,000 to 4,000 words per day, bringing their average daily bits of communication to around 7,000 units, if you include body language and other noises. But it is equally important to point out that other scientists, in an attempt to replicate their findings, could not.

One study in particular examined 396 participants in 2007 by having them wear a voice recorder that recorded ambient sounds for several days. Matthias Mehl, of the University of

Arizona, was a member on a team of researchers who found instead that both men and women used about 16,000 words.[19] Yet if you stopped 20 women randomly on the street and asked how many of them felt that their husbands talked as much as they did, the feedback you would receive would not support a 50/50 spread on the word count; more women than men complain about having silent partners (we know this is true because we conducted this experiment).

So how do we account for the discrepancy, and why are research results so contradictory? I believe the answer lies again in the categorization of the samples studied along gender lines. According to XY theory, either men or women can be the talkers (X types) or the more silent types (the Ys), so this would have had a cancelling effect (or more accurately what scientists refer to as a "moderating effect") on the results. Moreover our experience with clients at the Institute showed that X type men were quite likely to participate in an experiment regarding communication habits, whereas Y-type males often wouldn't even show up to take the XY test. Could it be that the Matthias Mehl study naturally attracted more X-type men, who were more likely to agree to such a study and would be natural talkers, thereby skewing the results?

According to our research, X type women and men talked and shared more during their day than their Y type partners did, and they hoped their partners would reciprocate. If an

X type woman does not meet her quota by the end of the day, she will seek interaction with her significant other, who may already have met his. If he is a Y type communicator, he is likely to do anything in his power to avoid that interaction, feeling spent, having used up his resource of words. Again, what makes this phenomenal are our findings at the Research Institute, where several hundred X types and Y types showed this disparity in communication as occurring not between men and women, but between X and Y personality types, whether male or female. Differentiation along gender lines blurred when their personality types were compared.

Actions Speak Louder Than Words, Except When They Don't

As children, we've been told by our parents that actions speak louder than words. This was their honest attempt to get us to realize that when they asked us to do something such as chores around the house, carrying out their request meant more to them than our simply promising to do so. So we grew up believing that actions do speak louder than words. But this is not true in an XY world. In reality, to the X type individual, words matter more. Not just specific types of words, not even just "sweet" talk such as "I love you," "You mean the world to me," "My life was so different before I met you," and so forth,

but everyday words. Social conversation, sometimes mean-
ingless words and nonfunctional, purposeless chatter, will do
the trick. Yes, it may seem sad that the conversation bar for X
types is set so low, but it is true.

As an X, you bond by talking. Previous concepts have
expressed the notion that it makes you feel better to vent, but
you know it's much deeper than that. You actually connect with
your partner by talking to him or her, and his or her refusal to
interact in this way creates distance, a void, an unwelcomed
feeling of rejection in the pit of your stomach. You know it
makes no sense that you should feel rejected simply because
your partner forgot to say good morning or good night, or continues to forget to ask how your day was. But we have found
that just the act of talking—not heavy, functional conversation, necessarily, but simply asking how someone's day was,
or sharing about your day, or calling during the day to say,
"How's it going? I miss you"—all greatly strengthen the bond.
Such efforts show that a partner cares and increase that
feeling of togetherness, of connectedness—the absence of
which creates problems in a relationship and begins to jeop-
ardize a marriage. And that is only the communicative scale.
We haven't even touched on the emotions or intimacy scale.

When we first started our research, we were convinced
that communication was the only factor giving rise to only two
personalities: X types and Y types. It was not until several

months later and over hundreds of tests administered, that we discovered not only were women extremely distressed by husbands who refused to talk, but quite a number of men felt the same about their wives. The discoveries for our research team did not stop there.

X type after X type kept at us to pay closer attention to the emotional scale. We had a few items on the original test that asked about emotions, and some of them still exist in the revised version, which you'll see in an abbreviated form in chapter 11. But we soon noticed that even when some X types had companions who communicated adequately, they continued to complain about feeling completely unfulfilled and disconnected. This discovery gave birth to the XY personality, where the first letter (X) refers to the communication need, and the second letter refers to the need for intimacy.

XY types are the individuals who communicate just fine, but not on an emotional level (as the "Y" in the XY designation indicates), and not in a way that expresses affection, gives attention, or offers emotional validation or support. One woman complained that she had not been hugged or kissed by her husband in decades and somehow something inside of her had died. Her husband told her she was overreacting, but the scientific research we will present in chapter 12 (The Chemical Affair), shows that she was not. However, the same research will explain why he couldn't easily appreciate how she felt about a seemingly inconsequential need. She would nag him about it for over 20 years before she would finally give up. It seems that communication is not our only need, but also a host of secondary needs that contribute to feelings of intimacy with our partner. Among those needs are empathy, attention, accountability, public display of affection, verbal expressions of emotion (which we call VEE), romantic gestures, and helpfulness. We will take a look at these secondary needs in chapter 5.

Chapter 4

What X Types Want

*O*ur research shows that X types tend to stay in a relationship longer than they should; long enough to take a blow to their self-esteem. If the Y partner keeps speaking the right words—making empty promises but using communication, the currency that matters most to an X—his X type partner will continue to keep hope alive, stay put, and believe her Y's promises to change. This occurs even in the face of all evidence to the contrary. As we mentioned in the previous chapter, we have historically been told that actions speak louder than words, and for the most part it's true. In XY relationships, however, applying the cliché is more complicated. What happened with this next couple below highlights this fact:

Jeffrey and Nicole were together for two years and fought fiercely for the better part of the second year. She had two primary complaints, neither of which had to do with commitment anymore, as they planned to be married within a year. First, she thought he could help a bit more around the house. Actually, they lived together in a small two-bedroom apartment, but this was home (We'll cover cohabitation in chapter 13). Secondly, she wanted children and he did not. But let's get back to the domestic help he wasn't giving. She knew that her managing the two-bedroom apartment was not excessive, but they both had full-time jobs, and he got home about two to three hours before she did. There was no reason why, in a modern world, he would think that he was right to let her do all the work, she thought. She could not see the logic or the fairness in his division of labor.

After much nagging from her, he gave in and agreed to wash the dishes after she cooked and cleaned. This was not agreeable to her, but she figured, better a little than nothing at all. She did *not* suffer in silence, however. Some personalities would suffer quietly (like Y type partners) and not let their significant other know exactly what was bothering them. But she was no Y, so she continued to complain almost daily. He called it nagging. She called it "speaking up, speaking my mind." She also felt that he avoided her by joining a bowling league that required him to be gone for hours every Sunday even though, because of their work schedules, they had only weekends together.

One day, Nicole stopped nagging. She stopped talking about the relationship. Hers wasn't even the silent treatment her boyfriend doled out frequently to show his displeasure. Those lasted a few hours and then life was back to normal. But this was not what she was doing. She suddenly seemed indifferent and, not having seen this in her before, he felt a bit nervous, scared. That night, Jeffrey went online and bought two tickets to Vegas, made reservations at the Paris Hotel, and had every intention of proposing to her there. If a ring was what she always wanted, he was about to make her dreams come true. They would make the trip in four weeks. During that time, he would not only clean the apartment regularly but also cook, mop, and sweep. He reduced his bowling bouts to only twice per month, missing two weekends and infuriating his team.

Once in Vegas, he sneaked off to the jewelry store and bought a two-carat diamond ring which he brought to dinner that night.

He recounted to her all of the changes he had made, but she just shrugged a shoulder. Her response? "That's nice, Jeff."

"So how much do I mean to you?" he said, quite unsure of himself now.

"What do you mean?" she asked, flatly.

"What do I do to prove myself?"

"To prove what, Jeff?" she asked.

"To prove everything. To prove how much I want to be with you, how much I've changed."

She shook her head. "It's over, Jeff. I'm finished. You're too late." Nicole threw the napkin on the table and stormed out of the restaurant, leaving Jeff touching his jacket pocket with the $6,000.00 diamond engagement ring inside.

When Jeff came to see me at the Research Institute, he was still confused. He had no idea why she left him, no idea what he'd done, and certainly no idea why he was unable to convince her to stay. After about an hour, I finally convinced him that *to him*, actions speak a lot louder than words, but not to her. As far as he was concerned, he had done everything he could possibly do to turn things around. But really, there was only one thing she wanted. She wanted him to call her more during the day; to *talk* to her more than he did. That was it. That was all. And he couldn't do it.

In earlier days, whenever they were apart, most often when he was away to visit family in Florida, she needed to hear from him more, but he came up short. It wasn't that she didn't trust him. The way she saw it though, he still had a huge *accountability* problem and he never seemed to understand that. To him, she was grossly overreacting. He had done more than most men. But, had he? In fact, in two years, he never once told her how he felt about her or came clean about the fact that he *didn't* think he could live without her. He could tell me over and over, choked up with emotion, but he couldn't tell her, and now she was gone.

Doctor X

In 2008, I jotted down the thoughts of two doctors: a doctor of theology and a doctor of dental surgery. The theologian shared with his congregation that when he talks to his wife, she doesn't always answer him. Nor does she answer him when he asks a question, at least half of the time. He explained that he had to get used to this aspect of her personality early in the marriage. He also hypothesized that the reason she takes a long time to answer or didn't do so at all is that she needed time to "process" before she responded, whereas he did not. I didn't know quite how to take this. Was he saying she was not as smart as he was or…that she was just slow at thinking things through?

If I were not a licensed psychologist in my previous line of work, I might not have known that processing speed, or a measure of how you process sensory information, has been seen as a component of intelligence for years. The higher the IQ, the faster you were thought to process data, similar to a computer with more RAM that can handle not only faster processes but multiple transactions at once, allowing you to have many programs open at the same time as you work on them simultaneously. Well, Y types, such as the minister's wife, generally do not process answers to relational questions particularly fast and do not enjoy multitasking, multi-tracking, multi-talking or multi-anything for that matter on topics of little interest or that serve no particular function. Though it is likely that she and other Y type mothers would take me to task for the multitasking comment, as women have practiced for cen- turies to carry a baby on one hip, and a broom or mop in one hand while tending to dinner on the stove with the other. Scientists who study what goes on in the brain will tell you that some tasks can improve with practice, but not all. But XY theory holds true, particularly with conversations, and espe- cially for Y types, as we mentioned before.

I don't know of any brain studies on the difference between the mental processes of X types vs. Y types, but suffice it to say, I have subjected willing clients, friends, and family members to IQ tests simply because they were Y types, and because I too was very curious about the slow processing. Those with IQs in excess of 130 (gifted levels) were just as slow at processing answers if the questions I asked, outside of the IQ testing, seemed mundane, relational, or uninteresting to them in any way. Several Ys admitted that they weren't even listening to the question, let alone attempting to formu- late an answer.

I mentioned two doctors, didn't I? So I'll have to say something about the other. He was a doctor of dental surgery (DDS). He was my personal dentist, and on one of my visits, he thought he could distract me from the pinch of the Novocain-filled needle by making small talk. He knew I was a psychologist and proceeded to explain that he had to hurry with my filling because his wife insisted they see a therapist in a small group session so he could learn to communicate better. She complained that he didn't talk enough. I nodded knowingly but didn't share anything about XY theory. He needed to learn to communicate *more*. She thought he needed to learn to communicate *better*. Two doctors. Two men. But one was an X in an XY relationship and the other, a Y, was enduring the same effects of a mismatch.

Immunity and Empathy

We will cover emotions and intimacy in the next chapter in greater detail. But if you are a Y type person partnered with an X type, you need to know that your partner's perception about how you "care" for the one you love, your X type partner, will differ from your own perceptions. Xs will doubtless have many more emotional crises than you would have as a Y, and the farther apart you are on the intimacy scale, the more distance there will seem to be between you, and the more emotionally reactive your partner will appear to you. Situations will arise that you will feel require no response, or at least not the size of the response you observe in your partner, and you will be surprised and dismayed. On this point, you could be tempted to downplay the importance of the event, whether it is the loss of a job, an argument with a coworker or relative, or the illness of a child.

Chances are that you are correct about the overreaction of your X type partner, but the relationship will benefit from your careful and considerate handling of his or her emotions at that point. I've spent the better part of this chapter encouraging you to communicate more with your X type partner. I've implied that you should utilize small talk more often and explained why talking more would help you to bond more, but this is the exception to all of that. When your partner is sharing emotionally—or more accurately, is emotional while sharing sensitive feelings—it would be best to be an active listener. Simply nod and make eye contact to let him or her know two things—you're listening and you care. In any event, if you are not a communicator, her adding emotion to the mix is certain to make your coming up with the perfect reaction that much more difficult. What she or he needs now is empathy. Don't look away or stare at your partner incredulously, don't look at your Blackberry™ or check your iPhone™ and don't do as so many Ys have admitted to doing, and walk away or leave the house. This is not the time to run away to seek your solitude, even if every pore and fiber in your body screams at you to do so. Stand your ground. Quietly. Lovingly. It'll blow over before you know it.

Francine

When Francine got off the phone with her mother, she was so visibly upset that her husband, Travis, swore he could see steam coming from her nostrils. Francine was having another one of what her husband called "her stupid conversations." Francine's mother and father were retirees who emigrated from Italy years ago and now resided in Philadelphia to be close to their daughter. Her parents used to live in the "old country" and loved and missed their Christmases in Tuscany (who wouldn't?). The problem however, was that they wanted to go to Italy for Christmas but waited too long to book a flight; now, just weeks before departure, in the height of the Christmas season, tickets would cost over $3,000.00—twice what they could have cost even three months earlier. When Francine's mother called the first time to complain about how her husband (Francine's dad) waited until the last minute to book the tickets, Francine agreed they cost too much and mentioned they should wait and travel outside of the busy

Christmas season. Francine's mother got angry and felt her daughter was out of line to say so.

The conversation took place repeatedly for three weeks, with Francine getting off the phone, angry with her mother every time. On the final and most heated of the arguments, she hung up the phone and asked Travis what he thought, as he sat at the table within earshot, listening to what was being said. He tried to say what he thought any husband should, but the words that flew out of his mouth, were anything but what he intended. He blurted, "You're having one of those stupid conversations again. You would think after listening to your mother's empty ranting for the 30 years you've been her daughter, you would learn to get used to her and simply ignore her."

"So you think I'm wrong?" Francine asked.

"You really want my opinion on that?" he fired back.

"Of course! Why would I ask if I didn't?"

"Well, I think you're right, but that's beside the point," Travis said.

"Beside the point? But it is the point! I have been putting up with these attacks from my mother for years whenever I try to help, and I'm tired!"

"If you've been doing it for decades, why aren't you *immune* to it by now? Why can't you just ignore her and let it go?"

Travis wasn't speaking about something he knew nothing about. He, too, had a father who criticized him weekly and was disappointed that he became a school teacher of elementary school kids, no doubt, instead of joining the family law firm. So he heard the criticisms and personal attacks enough to understand what his wife was going through. What he did not understand was why the same criticism would continue to trigger the same emotional response in his wife for so many years. It seemed to him that his wife was developing thinner emotional skin over time, causing her to become more and more reactive emotionally, while he was developing thicker skin in dealing with his own parent critic and had learned to tune his father out almost completely.

But these are not the underlying issues here. The key issue here is that Francine was not feeling the emotional support from her husband that she believed she needed. Not the immediate validation from her partner that said she was right and her mother was wrong. Not arguments put forward in her favor. Not a simple hug that would have said, "I care. I'm here for you." In fact, there was nothing in Travis's affect (or countenance) as he played on his laptop that indicated or registered either mild interest or a lover's concern. He never got up to go to her and was, for the most part, emotionally unresponsive, she thought. When she sought his opinion, he said in effect, "Just get over it."

To my Y friends reading this, I must say that this isn't about who's right and who's wrong: it's about empathy and voluntarily offering a more sympathetic response. You might never understand why your X type partner responds so emotionally to seemingly "little" things, but to be fully empathetic, you don't have to. It is important that Xs have emotional support, if not empathy, from their lovers. The next time similar incidents occur, before telling your partner about his or her overreaction, first explain that you understand. Remember, what triggers the meltdown might be intellectual, but your partner's response is emotional. Resist the urge to use your well-reasoned arguments. You might have noticed they seldom work on these occasions.

X types often complain about problems in an intellectual way, which, on the surface, seems to require a similar type of reasoning to squelch it. But the next time this occurs, say, "I'm sorry this happened, but I love you no matter what they say, no matter how much they try to upset you," and see the change in your partner's reaction. X types respond to emotionally supportive feedback, especially unsolicited. Your partner would probably respond to a hug or a reassuring hand squeeze while this "attack" is occurring. Sometimes you need not say a word. In fact, you can continue in silence, as long as you find a way to show that you care and are there for him or her. When it comes to needing empathy, your X type partner (unlike you) may never be self-sufficient, during the small or large incidents that trigger emotional reaction, and she or he will not get used to your unemotional approach when those triggers occur.

The way immunizations or vaccinations work, as you know, is that the immune system is activated or stimulated by introducing an inactive form of the virus or pathogen to enable the individual's body to develop adaptive immunity to the disease. The bottom line is that the individual's stimulated immune system is able to fight the next attack from the viruses; we call the process immunization, and it is one of the great accomplishments of modern science. However, the fact that Ys appear to be immune emotionally is not advantageous to the relationship.

When applied to XY theory, Y types have boasted about learning to be less trusting, if not sometimes downright distrustful, after one relationship that resulted in their hurt or some pain. Walls were immediately and sometimes unconsciously constructed for their emotional protection, their immunity. It is the immunity and the wall of protection that causes the Y types to be so fearful of commitment. That is why they are reluctant to open up, and are so hard and unreachable, or *unreadable*, by their X partners. It is the very absence of emotional immunity that causes X type individuals to be more vulnerable, but also more able to trust, to love, to be flexible and adaptable, and to make a relationship work, even with the most rigid of Y types. Most X types never talk of such walls, and when they exist for an X type, it comes only after considerable and recurring pain.

Chapter 5

Secondary Needs

*H*ow long would you stay in a relationship before your significant other said, "I love you" for the first time?

I have asked this question of countless individuals, and the responses are inconsistent. So let me ask you, how long would you stick around in the relationship waiting to hear those magic words? How long would it be before you began to feel insecure, unwanted, and maybe even unloved? One month? Six months? Maybe one year? Or is that too soon? Well, let me tell you about Frank, because Frank waited patiently for three years; Frank assumed he could tell for certain that his girlfriend, Denise, loved him by the way she treated him.

I visited the couple on several occasions. I saw Denise in action, cooking for him, cleaning the house without help, and serving him meals on a tray with silverware on white linen, while he clamored for her to do *less*—probably because he was unnecessarily concerned about how it would look to me. Still, it took Frank three years to be concerned about the fact that sometimes the disparity between what someone *does for* you, and what someone says they feel for you is so vast— that when you confront it, you could begin to doubt what your eyes have been telling your heart for years. Frank thought that his girlfriend had a difficult time with verbal expression of emotions (VEE). Not with feeling the emotion, just the expression of it. This condition includes being able to comfortably make statements such as "I care about you" or "I love you." He didn't know what the phenomenon was called, but he felt that whatever it was, she struggled with it, and he wouldn't hold it against her.

So he took his own dare, and quite spontaneously one evening, while on the way out of a movie theater, when he was feeling amorous after seeing a romantic movie, he turned to face her and put his arm around her shoulder. She was looking lovingly into his eyes; he was looking deep down into hers. He would ask her a serious question in a closed-ended and perhaps rhetorical way. He would make it as easy as possible for her to say—yes. So he said, "You love me, don't you?" In fact, he thought all she had to do was nod. That was all. He was quite prepared to accept that after three years. Just one nod.

But Denise didn't nod and didn't answer. So he asked the question again. He had previously dated a Y type female for four years and knew quite well that many times, several questions were interpreted as rhetorical and went unanswered. So he wasn't panicking . . . yet. He would ask again. And again— the answer was silence. "Oh, my goodness," he said, finally raising his voice in frustration. "So, you don't love me?"

This time she shook her head and said, "I can't answer that."

If you are a Y type emotionally, you might be wondering what this fuss is all about. Many Y types have little or no need for verbally expressed emotions (VEE). In fact, as I mentioned earlier, when XY testing began five years before this writing, the intimacy or emotional scale did not exist. However, the communication scale did, and it is still referred to as the primary scale when it comes to the XY concept. The reason is that all test items that factor into the communication score are items that relate closely to various aspects of a couple's communication. The secondary scale, on the other hand, covers more of a variety of items, including emotional items, and is often referred to as the emotional or intimacy scale. However, as we will soon learn in this chapter and the next, it truly covers more than just emotional factors. What's more, the items still communicate how one person feels about another...but they were missed by my team for years.

It took me two mixers (XY parties where individuals can match and mingle), and many explanations from several women about what they were dealing with, to realize that the XY Personality test should really comprise two scales: a communication scale and an emotional needs scale. Emotional needs are referred to as secondary needs, but not secondary in importance like we first thought. These needs are "secondary" because they're a composite of traits that factor into one score (intimacy), whereas in the communication scale, all questions are intended to measure the same construct—communication. But it is important to note that whenever secondary needs showed up on the scale as a low score, they created as much disillusionment and unfulfillment as a low score on the communication scale.

What you need to remember, when it comes to secondary needs, is that a number of emotional and other needs create problems in a relationship and cause individuals to feel unloved. It is important also to note that even Y types have secondary needs that factor into their feelings. Even though some of the individual items are not *emotional* in nature, they, too, facilitate bonding with partners. Let's begin with the list for X types:

- Affection
- Attention

- Affirmation
- Connectedness
- Accountability
- Verbal Expression of Emotion (VEE)
- Romance
- Public Display of Affection (PDA)
- Helping / Fairness
- Giving and Surprising / Reciprocity
- Proximity
- Value
- Empathy / Sensitivity
- Public Display of Emotion (PDE)

Affection: As it turns out, human touch—a soft embrace, a kiss, even a light squeeze—communicates, "I care, I love you; you matter to me." In the absence of these small expressions and displays, people tend to feel alone, detached, disconnected, and even taken for granted. One woman complained that she got more affection from her roommate in college than she did from her husband.

Attention: As far as emotions go, attention is more subtle. It does not require conversation, and a partner's laser focus isn't necessary, but there's something in how someone moves around you and about you that tells you she's attentive to you.

You get the sense that if you stubbed your toe or made a misstep, she would be right there to hold you and prevent your fall. In a crowded room, you can sense that the attentive lover still keeps you in peripheral view as you scoop from the punch bowl at a party or reach for the hors d'oeuvres. Like a mother who can recognize the cry of her infant in a crowded day care, you're certain that he or she would be there at your side at a moment's notice if need be. You're not afraid that the conversation you started might bore him to death, and you're certain that if it did, he wouldn't go out of his way to show it, or worse yet, to say it. You don't have to tell him that you're coming down with a cold. He sometimes notices it before you do. You might just find out you're coming down with something as he steps through the front door with a bag in hand of medicine he bought from the pharmacy. The back rub comes when you need it, often before you have to ask for it. If there's one person in the world who knows what you need and when you need it, and is there with it right on time, it's the attentive lover.

Affirmation: "I love you because I'm here." That's what he said when Martha asked her husband when was the last time he told her he loved her.

He went on to say, "I don't see why I have to keep saying that. You know I do. Why do I have to keep saying it?"

She said, "Why do I have to keep cooking? Why do I have to keep cleaning? Why do I have to keep raising your children? Why do I continue to iron your clothes? You say that actions speak louder than words, so I continue to show by my actions. Why can't I hear the words? I know you love me, but why can't you tell me every now and again? I need to hear that you still love me, to know that you still do. People change their minds every day, you know."

Let's go back to Martha's husband's first statement. Note, he didn't say, "*I'm here because I love you.*" The response still would not be ideal, but she would've accepted that. What he said was, "I love you because I'm here." Translation? I didn't have to be here. You should accept my presence, the fact that I'm still in your life, as you being fortunate that I'm still in your life. I must love you if I am. At least, that's how she took it. It's a typical response from Y types who want to avoid saying, "the words."

Would Martha's husband's response have been enough for you?

Accountability: When Tisha announced to her boyfriend that she needed to visit with her parents over a long weekend, Tommy didn't answer. She knew that he heard her because he always did. She had grown used to living in his rhetorical world. She wasn't about to ask him for the 500th time: "Did you hear what I said?" Or keep wondering whether he had thought that it didn't require a response. She knew that to him, it did not. After four years of marriage, she knew him well, or so she thought, until her plane flew off into the sunset and she called him five hours later to let him know that she had arrived at her destination safely. And if this story sounds similar to others that I've shared, or will share, it is because it happens over and over to XY couples. I call it the "accountability" problem. Needless to say, Tisha went an entire weekend without hearing from her man. She became hysterical and worried the entire time that she was visiting with her family. When she returned home, a fight ensued. But accountability is such a huge point of contention in XY couples that relationships have ended because of it. Not domestic abuse or infidelity, but "accountability," with surprising frequency.

VEE: This is an acronym for Verbal Expression of Emotion and it's not just the three words, "I love you," that Y types struggle to say. They also struggle to say how much their partners mean to them or that life would seem empty without them. Hallmark moments come with difficulty for Y types. So they often find it easier to text their emotions. Others can more easily communicate by e-mail, and still others exhibit an old-fashioned flair with use of snail-mail. So, my X type friends, check to see if your companion has a preferred medium to communicate how he feels about you, and you just might find out for the first time, how much positive emotion he still has for you; how much care he has locked up in that heart for you, just waiting to find a medium of expression. But, where words fail, romance often succeeds.

Romance: There's no doubt that we live in a romantic age. It is scarcely necessary to tell you what romance is, but keep in mind that if emotionally, you're a Y type, your X type partner is struggling daily to see signs that you still care. She needs words and some romance to bond and to connect, and sending her off to bond with her girlfriends so that you can have more free time, has not been cutting it. Girlfriends are not a substitute for the love of a man, and if she's not getting words—your loving words— and you're more a man of action, then where are the romantic acts?

Y type men and women must step it up. This one doesn't even require faking. She's not going to wonder what you were thinking when you send her a dozen roses. She's not going to question your true motives. That's the nice thing about romance. It speaks for itself and stands on its own. Romance always means only one thing: I'm really into you, and I cared enough to try. Granted, there are times that we mess up and romance says, "I'm sorry," but the person who says, "I'm sorry" is very often a person who still cares.

PDA (Public Displays of Affection): When Christina took a walk one afternoon with Danny, she accidentally let her hand touch his as they walked down the boardwalk at the beach to the water's edge, to stare at the sunset. He felt the tentative brush of her fingers and grabbed her hand, squeezed it gently, but held onto it. She smiled sheepishly and asked, "Do you want your hand back?"

"No," he said, grinning, "Why would I? We've been dating now for four months. I was wondering what took you so long. It's OK. I enjoy holding hands."

She looked surprised. "Really? In a public place like the beach? There are hundreds of people around here."

"I don't care if someone sees us holding hands," he said, convincingly.

She seemed flushed with emotion. "I, I just can't remember when last, public displays of affection were OK with a guy, with any guy I've ever dated."

And as Christina briefly described the guys she had been with, they all seemed to consistently be Y types. So she had to adjust over time, forgetting all she knew, erasing who she was before, or rather what she was forced to become, when she was conditioned by her ex-boyfriends. She enjoyed this so much more. She had to dial back and find it again. But she wasn't done with the reflection.

"My ex didn't care about me. He only cared about what happened to himself. He cared about his image. I always got the impression that we were hiding from someone, like he had a secret life. A Witness Protection Program or something. But, somewhere, deep down inside, I knew he didn't. He just didn't like PDA."

Helping/Reciprocity/Fair Play: This is a big one. And this is probably a creation of our modern age. In many homes today, both parents must work just to make ends meet. Traditionally, the woman stayed at home and became the homemaker. The man went out and worked and brought home the bacon…but something happened in the last 60 years. Women went out to work and then came home and worked some more with little or no help from the men. This does not seem like an XY issue, does it? So why is it on this list? It's on this list because both X and Y type women interpret a non-helping man as a man who does not care about them—but for very different reasons. For the Y partner who is not helped, an unspoken contract is being broken, violated. His or her X partner is showing by actions that he or she does not care. The Y partner is likely to have negotiated for a division of labor, even along traditional lines, such as the man working in the yard and the woman in the house, as long as he or she is not slacking off. The Y partner who is overworked will likely talk about how unfair it is.

The X partner would be more likely to tolerate symbolic help and would love to work together with her partner, to work with him side by side, or at least at the same time, if possible. Helping is sharing. X types are into fair play but are more tolerant of an *attempt* at fair play than Y types. If her Y partner did less, that's OK. At least he's with her in the kitchen, perhaps even talking to her and being a companion. With the X, proximity goes a long way. She needs a demonstration of his love and affection. Suggesting he get a maid to relieve her is more likely to appeal to the more functional Y type female than to the X type, who may see this as an attempt to get out of family share time, unless he can convince her that this is being offered so that time can be freed up to allow them to spend more quality time together later. Sharing is a form of communication, and subsequently, bonding, which is also the problem with the man who wants to come home and sit and watch TV alone while she does all the work.

Giving and Surprising: This gets its own section separate from romance because of a nuance of a difference. Leaving little surprises, tucking away little notes, packing a small suitcase and stealing your loved one away for a weekend, buying the tickets to her favorite concert so she can enjoy her favorite male artist—the same one she knows you don't really like—takes romance to another level. Scientists tell us that for the

Y, it fills the need for novelty, which produces some of the same hormones that were released when you were a new couple and gave rise to the feeling of falling in love. Surprises work for both Xs and Ys, but surprise activities (as opposed to say, little notes) seem to be the Y preference. Where reciprocity becomes an issue for the X type woman is after years of giving and not receiving from the Y type man, whose attitude often is summed up by the words, "But I didn't ask you to do any of that."

Connectedness: Everything that has gone before this point in this chapter leads to the answer to this one question: Does your partner feel connected or disconnected, attached or detached from you? In Volume II, we talk about the five stages of an extreme (XY) relationship. The final stage of an XY relationship is withdrawal or disconnection, when a couple steps into what is called an ambiguous relationship. It's what happens in the absence of all the things we spoke about previously—when there's no longer any affection and it is clear that there is lack of care; when she has given up on securing affirmation of her man's love; when she ceases to feel secure about what he's doing; when he won't stay in touch during their times apart. It can also occur when she can see and hear him express himself emotionally to others, including the children; it's the fact that he just could not muster the same level of emotion for her. At that point, whether she leaves or stays, love has died.

Proximity: Proximity is a secondary need of X types, particularly emotional Xs. As an X, you enjoy doing things with your partner and love to be in close proximity even if you're not engaging in conversation. You almost never feel that you need a time-out from being around your significant other. You never tire of him or her. You never need a break from him or her. If you feel you do, your intimacy score is not as high as you thought. Moderate Xs and High Xs generally do not have a proximity problem with each other, but if you find yourself with a Y type partner, he will need time and space for no reason other than that it's his personality. In fact, it's a need of his, if he's truly a Y. You must try to accept that fact and not take that need personally. It's not about you. We've already talked about your need for accountability from your partner, but Y types, in general, are not accountable. When you combine their need for time away from you with their inclination to not want to stay in touch during their alone time, any insecurities you might have about your partner are likely to surface in this scenario and be worsened by it.

Value: X types often complain about not feeling *valued* in a relationship and of being "taken for granted" by their Y type partners. In fact, use of that particular phrase, "taken for granted," is often a signal that they are in an XY relationship. What Xs are really saying when they itemize the things they've done for the family—the marriage or relationship, and most of all the significant other—is that they're not feeling loved. According to XY speak, this is another way of saying, "I don't feel connected to you like I used to, or like I would like to." In addition to saying that, X types can also say, "I feel you don't care about me. I feel you don't cherish me. I feel you don't care about this relationship."

Words such as "acknowledged" or "gratitude" are even less direct ways to bring up the topic of value when you consider that for Y types, actions are the currency of a loving bond, while "words" will do it for X types. So complaining about not being recognized for the things she does would seem out of character for an X. It's a substitution that she (or he) expects will work, but it often falls short of conveying the true sentiment, which goes something like this: "Hey, man, you haven't told me you loved me since my birthday...three years ago, and we haven't gone out romantically for a year. What's going on?"

Empathy/Sensitivity: This need or trait is tricky and closely related to the need we'll discuss next. Have you ever gotten yourself into a difficulty, suffered a loss, or gone through something really painful but felt that the person or persons you shared your loss with could not care less? They didn't come out and really *say* it. They weren't openly mean and might have even given you a hug or said the right words, but you could sense the emptiness behind the gesture. Some people genuinely have a difficult time empathizing with others or putting themselves in the other person's shoes. Scientists have a name for that. They call it "theory of mind." Individuals with Asperger's Syndrome (an Autism Spectrum Disorder) have difficulty understanding how someone else feels. They have difficulty with what is called pragmatic (social) language as well. They won't be able to read your facial expressions as you share how you feel. They won't be able to "feel your pain" and, if they did, could not verbalize an empathetic response without sounding robotic and detached. It is interesting to note that hormones and other chemicals in the brain are under suspicion for playing a role in that condition in children with autism—but when scientists wanted to test the hormone, dubbed by many researchers as the "cuddle" or bonding hormone, they performed their test first on a group of men. They gave them pre- and post-tests on empathy, before and after administering the hormone, to see what effects it might have.

The men became more empathetic after the drug was administered (but were expected to make a full recovery to their usual un-empathetic selves as soon as the drug wore off). The drug also made them more communicative. So plans are already underway for testing on children with autism. The effect hormones and genetics play on your partner's relationship behavior will be covered more fully in a later chapter (The Chemical Affair!). Remember also to apply XY theory to everything, especially any studies that state that "men" have behaved in ways our research suggest to be typical of Y types. We will then assume that for some, the old paradigm is still in effect but will reinterpret the study's results accordingly.

Sensitivity, closely linked with empathy, is a complaint of Xs who charge that their Y partners are lacking in this area. It should come as no surprise that Y types have complained that their X types were *too* sensitive.

PDE (Public Display of Emotion): Well, not really "public." We're not talking here about the child who only waits until a trip to the store or mall to throw himself on the ground and have a tantrum for no reason at all, other than perhaps to embarrass his parents. By public, I mean not *privately. The X type person is comfortable displaying emotions* among family members, and certainly in the presence of their partner—someone they can feel free to cry in front of. Similarly, you might show worry and anxiety if your job is on the line. Your freedom to express these emotions and your partner's ability to match them with the appropriate response is very bonding. Sharing emotional experiences and moments fosters closeness for an X, and a Y type partner needs to be aware of this.

I know these are too many traits to remember, but there is no need to try to remember all of them. At the end of chapter 11, they will be presented again, and you will be asked to rate the level of your need for each characteristic. In chapter 11, we'll also describe the test you'll take in more detail and pull these concepts together. All of these items are contributing to your emotional score to be computed electronically, as to do it any other way would be extremely time consuming and complex.

The Secret Basket

Remember, in these chapters we are dealing with the secondary needs of both X and Y types. Though the scale used to measure it is considered a measure of a couple's intimacy or feeling of closeness, or more accurately, their need for intimacy, many of the traits identified in the test would not (when isolated) seem as good contributors to closeness at all. One such trait is "solitude." Considered by itself, it would seem odd that one's need for solitude, or "being left alone" from time to time, could actually bring a couple together and increase their connectedness. The concept of taking two entities further apart to bring them closer takes some effort to wrap our brain around it. And many X types have had to accept that fact by faith because it is what one Y after another said they needed. We'll call it the concept of "anti-traits"—traits that fundamentally represent the absence or the opposite of traits Xs need, but produce the similar result of closeness. It might also be that although these traits don't have the pulling, bonding effects of X traits, they at least do not push Ys away. We will see a similar brain teaser when we get to the next chapter on Y Needs and how their X type partners can improve their relationships with them.

The basket of secondary needs are all covered here in this chapter, but not exhaustively for X types. What is presented above are the needs we gleaned after testing hundreds of X type men and women—needs that have been identified as absolutely essential to their sense of connection to their partner and to satisfaction in the relationship. But beyond these, there is a "secret basket" with personal needs not included on our list. Even though we have isolated the most frequently mentioned needs, often an X type woman will have a special need peculiar only to her and perhaps to a few others. Until she shares it with others, it's her secret need. And until she shares it with her partner so he can attempt to meet that need, she cannot be fully "actualized," or fulfilled, in the relationship. That is, she won't feel happy or completely satisfied, and he is left to play a frustrating game of "guess the need."

Chapter 6

Y Needs

We will now turn our attention to Y mates. They, too, have secondary needs, but not emotional ones. Remember that many of their traits are anti-traits. They match those of their X counterparts but are the exact opposite. One such trait is the need for space, expressed exactly at times when Xs (especially emotional Xs) love togetherness and need proximity (or closeness). In the case of this anti-trait, it certainly will exhibit itself if you, as the X in the relationship, insist on forcing excessive closeness and togetherness to the point that your partner feels suffocated and pushed away.

Let's take a look at the Y's secondary needs. Notice that at face value, they are not emotional needs at all, though they foster bonding for Ys. They are as follows:

- Common Interests
- Solitude
- Time
- Space
- Actions
- Shared Activities
- Compatibility
- Novelty
- Privacy
- Loyalty / Unconditional Trust

Let's talk about these secondary needs of Y type personalities. As touched on in the next chapter, Y types bond in completely different ways than X types do. In fact, there may appear to be nothing emotional about the bonding at all, which explains in part why it seems easier for Y types than X types to walk away from a relationship. This isn't always the case, of course, as Ys are not as demonstrative as their X partners and would prefer not to express the pain and loss they may be experiencing. Nevertheless, more than a few jilted Xs complained of easily broken bonds. Their description paints a picture of Y bonding that resembles what you could find between two buddies at the gym—guys they're just hanging out with. So little emotion is shown when a long-lasting relationship formally collapses. The fact is there is an emotional component to Y bonding that is real, but different. Often, it's more cere-bral, more logical and calculated—but real, just the same.

Common Interests: This is the first of the secondary needs and is one of the primary ways Y type men in particular, feel bonded with their partners. If they share common interests when they meet, the closeness grows rapidly. They may both be into rock climbing or skydiving, maybe NASCAR races or even fishing or video games; whatever the common interest might be, they form a bond because of it. What this means is the X type partner who willingly assimilates Y type inter-ests will have an easier time forming the connections with her partner that she craves (we will go into this concept a little later). Unfortunately, the converse is also true. If she tended to be a more inflexible person, more independent, more adamant about focusing on her own interests—even within the context of the relationship—then the Y type partner is likely to take offense, to feel that his X type mate is somewhat uninterested in him (not just his lifestyle), and by extension, uninterested in bonding. Here is where many Xs fall into self delusion or find it necessary to practice social faking. Primarily to impress and bond with their love interest, they fabricate their interest in his favorite activities. This occurs particularly in the begin-ning—until later when quizzed about it, and they're exposed for the lies they've told, the lies they almost believed. They learn quickly that Ys take lying seriously, even if fabricating served the purpose of facilitating closeness.

Solitude: Many Y types require solitude. Remember this anti-trait? There are times when they simply want to be left alone. These times seem to correspond with a strenuous day; with the end of a long, hard, trying work week; or sometimes with a period of time during which they have some problem they're grappling with on a personal level. They would rather be left alone at these times. They're not big talkers and won't share information just for the sake of sharing. X types will share a problem and be comforted by doing so, whether a solution presents itself or not, because the exchange fosters bonding, brings the two closer together and is emotionally soothing. There is no such logic for Ys.

Conversing is not a method for bonding with Ys, and *not* for problem solving or brainstorming. If there is no chance that you might have a solution, there is no point in mentioning the issue to you. This tends to hurt X types, who feel slighted and ignored, excluded from a partnership in which ideally they believe all things should be shared. Xs want to be a part of the decision-making process. They have a brain and not just the hearts that they wear on their sleeves. You will not only *always* know what your X type is feeling on a regular basis, but you know what they're thinking as well, because this too, is publicized. It's the reason you, as the Y partner, think Xs talk too much. What you will only *think* about, they feel compelled to verbalize. For many X types, that's the only way *to* think. Aloud. So for them, it's hard to allow their Y partners the solitude that they need to process, but I would suggest that this is a skill worth learning and adopting.

Time: Matt and Olivia had been together for a year, but Matt was beginning to feel smothered. They did everything together, and one day Matt just wanted to get away, so he mentioned that he was going to the local Walmart™ to pick up a few things. Olivia quickly grabbed her jacket and asked if she could join him. "…Ummmm. I just need to be alone for a while," he said.

"I promise I won't bother you," Olivia countered, forcing Matt to raise his voice to repeat, "I said I need some time alone."

"I didn't think it was a big deal, Matt. I'll never bother you again or ask if I can come along for the ride."

"Well, as I said," Matt added, "I need to be alone." And with that, Matt was gone.

Olivia texted me at that moment to complain about Matt's need for time alone, and I chided her for making a big deal of his wanting to get away. She still didn't get it. She defended his need by explaining that perhaps he really wanted to get some stuff at Walmart, and it being the Christmas season, he didn't want her to see it. Maybe he was going to get her a gift or something. I explained that I didn't think that was it, in this case. I offered that perhaps if she were subtle but observant when he came back, she would notice that he had no bags whatsoever in his hands.

She was, and he didn't. But it didn't end there.

I asked her to observe, but she instead confronted. "So where are your bags, Matt?"

"What bag?" he asked, genuinely confused.

"Your bags. You went to Walmart, remember?"

"Oh. I didn't get what I wanted."

"OK," she said, finally getting it. "That's OK."

Y types need time alone, time away from the family, but time away from their over sharing X partners, in particular. They suffer from information overload so easily that even casual information shared causes communication overload for Ys and drives them to look for time, solitude, and space. Let's talk about space.

Space: There's no telling to what length a classic YY type person would go to get his or her space. I think the Y male in particular often tries to escape from everything that the X type female brings to the relationship, which must seem to him like a host of needs that he feels he is incapable of fulfilling. As an X type, you feel you're most alive and fulfilled when you're with him. Sorry to burst that bubble, but as many Ys have explained, they feel most rejuvenated, refreshed, and alive when they're alone with their own thoughts, in their own un-shared, un-compromised space. Yes, that would be—away from you.

To accomplish this, they'll do anything, come up with any reason or any excuse, to escape what feels like constant pressure. He'll ask to go on a hunting trip in another state, though he catches nothing; attend business workshops he didn't really need to attend; take family visits to see his mom or his six-month old cousin. One Y type man even told his live-in girlfriend that he had to take a weekend off so he could go to his mother's house to visit his dog that he missed a lot (and she bought his story, feeling that it was very "sensitive" of him).

At these times, he considers this his time off, and probably wants minimal contact with you because to be in constant contact defeats the very purpose of his trip. The X type female should examine what the previous few days were like for her partner just before he temporarily jumped ship. Was he being driven away by the overstimulation that comes with heavy con-versation, busyness, frivolous demands that lead to a stressful negative feedback loop, where a conflict is never resolved? (We'll talk more about loops in Volume II of XY Theory, when we deal with XY conflict.) Or, did you expose him to stories he'd heard before, or constant chatter that made even you tired of listening to your own voice? Remember that Y type men do not multitask (or multi-track) well, and not nearly as well as Y type women do. So maybe some adjustments need to be made so that he could have his space *within* the home, without feeling he has to seek it outside.

If he is a "sports" Y, (a Y type who uses sports to get away) and is using that TV time for his solitude and for space, are family members jumping all over him during his time? Does he need to take the long trip out of state because he's been denied the short trip to see his buddies at the sports bar on a Friday night? These are some of the questions a partner needs to ask, and some of the adjustments that can be made, just to cut down on his need for space. Remember, everything we do, whether X or Y, communicates something, and if he's asking for space, then you need to ask, "What is he really asking for and why?" and try and provide or adjust for just that, so that he stays.

Actions: This is the reason so many Y type men (and women) feel that it is OK to work a 70-hour week if they are doing so to provide a certain standard of living for the family. We learned that for Xs, words often speak louder than actions, but for the Y type male and female, actions speak louder than words. A simple mention that you would do something, complete some task—such as pick up his dry cleaning or take the dog to the vet—is treated like a promise written in blood. Any adjustment to what you promised to provide, including cleaning, meals, sex, and so forth, that looks like a withholding or change to the contract, is likely to make the Y type person angry or quietly resentful.

After all, Ys are keeping up their end of the bargain by being a provider or a homemaker—or possibly a father taking care of the yard, doing repairs to the home, and repairs at no cost. At this point, what's relevant is not how you feel but what you do. Division of labor means equitable division. What's relevant to your partner is whether you broke your word. So be very careful about your words. Although they come to you so freely, they should not be shared with the same gusto. Don't promise a thing to your partner that you know, deep down inside, you can't or possibly won't deliver.

The phrase "It's the thought that counts" means nothing to your Y type partner. Don't say, "We can go from having sex once a month to twice a week," knowing that you work a full-time job and are pretty much wiped out from taking care of the kids when you get home. His knowing that you will be very exhausted, perhaps too exhausted to perform, while he is exceedingly fresh and ready to go, will not save you from his inquisition. It is crucial that you always find out what the terms of your Y's *contractual* obligations for you are because these drive expectations, and expectations impact marital and relational satisfaction.

Shared Activities: These are not exactly the same as common interests. Having common interests allows you a topic of conversation, which typically fuels your non-conversational partner's interest. It is very often important to your Y type partner that his significant other share his interest. Naturally, this should be investigated and negotiated before getting into a commitment of marriage or any committed relationship. Shared activity however, takes "common interest" to the next level and, incidentally, the bonding as well.

When Leticia met Brent, it was intriguing that he drag-raced cars as a hobby. She loved talking to him about it. She tried to learn some of the jargon, and even bought a book for dummies on how to fix cars so she could understand his "car talk" better. She should have been given kudos for her efforts because she had done what many X type women might not have. But, to Brent, she still fell short. It would've clinched the deal for him if she had taken her interest to the next level—to the level of *activity*.

He had invited her at least a dozen times to his drag meets. After showing her the trophies he had won, he wanted to show her exactly how he did it. But she had no desire to go to the tracks and no desire to see him drive over 120 miles an hour. I thought I understood that she perhaps had the fear that many other spouses would have—the fear of seeing their loved one put his life at risk for a reward she would value less than his life. But the more I chatted with her, the more I realized she had no such fear at all. She simply had no interest in participating with him in this activity. That and some other things I detected when we spoke caused me to be curious enough to ask her to take the XY Personality test.

What I discovered was that this woman had a Y type personality. Y type women, as we will learn, are not assimilators, are not the most flexible people in the world, and do not always feel a pressing need to change to make a relationship work. Actually, she had done more than I would've expected of a Y, in doing what she did to learn about his hobby. But performing and engaging in it, was asking too much. Brent was also a Y type personality, and this is one of the few setbacks with Y types choosing Ys to be with in a committed relationship. One would expect it should be a match made in heaven. Instead, it is often fraught with pitfalls and potholes. We will talk more about the YY relationship in Chapter 9, when we look at Y type women.

Compatibility: Because Y types do not bond using the X types' communicative and emotional means, compatibility with their partners becomes more critical. On the other hand, an X type woman would adjust to suit the man she's with—so much so that if you were to see that XY couple years later, it is sometimes difficult to tell that they were a mismatched *extreme* couple with opposite scores on the XY continuum. We will cover these different types of couples in Volume II. For now, understand that extreme couples are on the extreme opposite end of the XY continuum or scale, with a configuration such as XX/YY. Y type men do not adjust well either, and, as a result, they are much better off finding someone who will adjust, such as an X or a Y higher on the scale and hence more adaptable. She should be assimilating to him in every way.

The tolerance of the Y's need for solitude is best achieved by an X who is really independent, who does not mind spending time away from her partner, who isn't insecure about her partner spending time on his own, and who values actions and believes that statements made should be given the same importance as rules and laws. These should be partners willing to participate in some shared activity, even if that activity might not be of initial interest to the X type partner.

It helps if all the other elements of compatibility are present, such as similar cultures, similar religion, similar values, and similar feelings about how money should be used. Other elements include how children should be raised, who should have control of the relationship, how conflicts should be handled, how much space should be allowed, and whether or not they value each other to the same degree. If these core elements of compatibility are met, then an XY relationship could resemble a harmonious match.

Novelty: Y types in particular crave novelty in the marriage, the feeling that everything hasn't grown stale. The most cited reason for ending marriage among Ys isn't infidelity but boredom. So plan trips to counteract this; even picnics in the park as an inexpensive option. The same goes for sex. It's just a shared activity to many Ys. Buy a few position books if you have to, in order to keep the bedroom alive. Whipped cream isn't only for strawberry pancakes. If you suck all the emotion out of the relationship, if there's no domestic help at home, and if she begins to think that she can do well enough by herself, there's a disconnect that often results in a separation. But it's difficult for a Y type to tell when his X partner has gotten to this point, because she fires so many salvos, gives so many warnings, that it's hard to tell which is the last warning. So I'll tell you in advance that when the nagging stops and the complaining ends, and you mistake her checking out of the relationship for her attempt to keep the peace, then you know you're in the final stage of your relationship and the die may already be cast.

Privacy/Loyalty/Unconditional Trust: Y types attempt to guard their privacy are legendary. More than a few X type partners have put their relationships in jeopardy by not adhering to their partner's code of secrecy and privacy. You are safer not sharing anything that occurs between the two of you with anyone, because it is impossible to discern what your Y partner will deem a breach of trust and loyalty if you did.

Chapter 7

The Y Type Personality

*R*esearch has shown that in addition to having huge deficits in their ability to communicate (as we discussed earlier), children with severe autism also generally show an unwillingness to be touched or cuddled, even by loving caregivers (parents, siblings, and teachers). More importantly, these children tend to be *instrumental* in how they relate, even to those who love them.

But I'd like to take a little time to explain the use of the term "instrumental." The word's connotation is that of someone with the ability to play an instrument: a guitar, maybe a piano. These instruments cannot play melodious music on their own, no matter how finely tuned they are. Nor can these instruments play the sounds they want to play when they want to, or for as long as they want to. They are at the mercy of their "owner," the guitarist or pianist, in this case. If the owner no longer wants the instrument, he can give it away, smash it, or trade it in for a better one—a newer one—the latest make or model.

Unfortunately, Xs have complained that their Y partners tend to use them instrumentally as well. Though I have interviewed at least a dozen women who told me in front of their partners that *they didn't mind being used* by them, the majority of X type women were not happy to learn of this Y trait. One Y man I tested and found to be an extreme Y told me that his grandmother, whom he swore was also a Y type, had told him that women were there to be used by him. He went on to explain that he was aware that he uses women, but he was raised to do so. Raised by a Y type guardian to use women! He is not in the majority, thankfully, and his view is extreme, but his treatment of the opposite sex is not unique.

Once we discussed the results, I was able to convince him that the reason he lived his life that way was probably not because his deceased grandmother, whom he loved dearly, had told him to do so. He was doing it because his personality predisposed him to do so, and the environment in which he was raised gave him the final push. Knowing his girlfriend well, and having her as a personal friend, I went the extra mile to encourage him to not view the women he dates as mere objects and to treat them with more respect, rather than as instruments to be played and later discarded.

It is important to note, though, that it would be as rare to see a musician crying over a guitar he traded in for a new one as it would be to see an extreme Y type lamenting his loss of an X type partner to whom he no longer felt attached and no longer cared to use, instrumentally.

Blueprints

So who exactly would Y types *not* use instrumentally? Well, someone who fits their blueprint.

The typical X type person would have a written checklist or blueprint of the type of guy she would want to marry, but would meet a guy, fall in love, and never bother to look at, or bring up that list again. The Y type man or woman, by contrast, would never write a list but would keep a mental blueprint of his or her perfect man or woman, never write any of it down, never talk about it or refer to it, but never veer away from it, except in the most dire of circumstances. Do you fit your Y partner's mold, his or her blueprint? Some Ys have been bold enough to tell their partners they weren't marriage material, after all. You'll just never know how honest (or blunt) your Y might be unless you ask.

The Letter

A woman I interviewed wrote a letter to her boyfriend at the end of a year-long battle of a relationship. It wasn't obvious to me that she was in an XY relationship at first, perhaps because of the duality we had, where I was both her friend and her interviewing/research psychologist. But the basics of what an X type typically wants were all mentioned in the letter. She talked about her unmet need for communication, affection and romance. It took her boyfriend almost two weeks to respond, though, and the letter was probably what provoked his disappearing act soon after. This is not the reaction we're hoping for when we reach out to our partners. So, let's take a look at what makes Ys tick.

Bonding

I was there the first time Ben came over to Lori's home, and I was probably invited so I could provide her with an informal personality assessment of her new friend. I cautioned Lori to avoid mentioning that I was a psychologist so her friend wouldn't be on his guard and show his best behavior. Clearly, that caution went unheeded. Yes, he admitted to being nervous about me being invited when she told him what I did for a living, as he sat in front of me. But that wasn't enough to prevent him from revealing to me—behind her back—that he had never been in love before and had never felt "connected with any of his ex-girlfriends." He was 36 and previously married. She was 30 and also a divorcee. I was certain he would add, "except with Lori," to his confession. Instead, this honest bloke told story after story, explaining how detached he could be after years of dating, making love to, and sometimes living with or fathering children with a woman. Later, I cautioned my friend that this was not a good sign, but she pointed out other positives, including how excited and passionate he was about her. I countered, "but he also said that he hadn't said 'I love you' to any of his ex-girlfriends!"

She answered, "But when the time is right, he'll say it to me." She was right. He said it and then broke off the relationship soon after (the first of four break-ups in 10 months).

It is startling to contemplate the number of Y types who remain in a relationship for years and feel nothing emotionally for the one they're with.

Another woman's boyfriend confided that he hadn't loved his ex that he lived with, and hadn't told her he loved her, even once, in 7 years.

Two days before this writing, a Y type woman I interviewed shared that she was planning to break it off with her boyfriend she had been with for 4 years. As I was about to offer solace, she said, "Oh, it's OK. I never really fall deeply in love with anyone I date anyway!" X types beware!

Maybe it's the fact that X type personalities bond by talking and touching, and true Y types, who are resistant to either— then are left without the proper mechanisms for deep bonding at the same level. The fact that your Y type is willing to stay with you is not necessarily a sign of either love for you or commitment to the relationship. When questioned in inter- views, many Ys extol a host of reasons to stay with signifi- cant others—reasons that can best be categorized under the heading of "convenience." However, this information might not be that important to many Xs. One 25-year-old woman asked me—after XY testing—what I thought about her results. When I told her that her partner might not have the depth of feelings for her that she might want, she responded, "But that is not what I'm asking you. Is he gonna leave me, or will he stay?"

It isn't that Y type men and women are incapable of bonding or attaching to someone with a different personality type. It's just that they do so in different ways and for different rea- sons. Whereas Xs bond by communicating, Ys have to "hang out" with you to bond. They bond through shared activity and shared experiences, which is why distance is the enemy of successful dating for XY couples. Granted, there are some Ys who are not the outdoors type, but there are activities indoors you can share. You may not like them, but it is important to share in them or you'll find yourself with an unhappy or bored Y on your hands. Prior to a break-up, an X would often talk about how disconnected she felt, and how much she and her partner drifted apart. Ys describe parting feelings differently. They typically talk about being bored to death, having out-grown their partner, or feeling suffocated. So joining in playing computer games or sitting and watching those TV shows with him could go a long way toward him feeling that you're still a "team."

One woman Facebooked with her husband because she knew he loved to communicate this way, even though he was upstairs and she was on the laptop downstairs in the same house. But Facebook™ was his "thing," so they made it work for them.

A study conducted on marital boredom and how it predicts, less satisfied partners 9 years later, sheds light on the XY phenomenon. The researchers interviewed 123 married couples in year 7 of their marriages, having given boredom plenty of time to creep in. The questions asked included, "During the past month, how often did you feel your marriage was in a rut, that you did the same thing all the time and rarely got to do exciting things together as a couple?" Another question had to do with how satisfied they were as a couple. The results indicated that *early boredom* in a relationship predicts marital dissatisfaction 9 years later.[20]

The experimenters suggested that marital boredom can be reduced by "shared participation in exciting activities." This effect is based on a "self-expansion model," which, according to the researchers, "indicated that the excitement often experienced during relationship formation arises from rapid development of closeness, the rate of which inevitably declines over time." The authors go on to point out that you can jump-start your relationship again and reignite the honeymoon-like passions by arranging for you and your partner to experience excitement from new and challenging sources, but in a "shared context."

Your lover can actually feel closer to you because you've fostered closeness and bonding by doing new, exciting things together. What this means is that you may have to give up the bake sale or bingo and join your husband as he coaches your son in Little League. So you thought those soccer moms were a bit intense, a little aggressive? Guess what? You might have to be on the sidelines screaming, "Goal! Goal! Goal!" pretty soon, if this is what will bond you with your husband and kids. And, of course, there is the option of joining him for a round of golf—even if you couldn't tell the difference between a hockey stick and a golf club. You might consider joining the country club with the very people you deride as stuffy and stiff, if this is what your boyfriend or husband is into.

But here's a word of caution: Be sure that your new foray into his world of activities is by invitation only, or he is likely to see it as an intrusion, an encroachment. Y types also need, not just time alone, but time away. Don't take this personally. It's how he copes with continuing to be happy in a close-knit relationship when deep down inside, every fiber of his being craves solitude. A quiet processor of information, as opposed to his more expressive and communicative partner, he can get a lot of processing done on the golf course or at the river with his fishing buddies, where more time is passed in silence, than he can get at home.

But also beware of missed hints. Whereas X types drop atomic bombs of information, Y type communication often resembles a fizzled, failed firework: just a small hint here, a suggestion there. It is not uncommon for divorcees to find out years later about activities husbands wanted them to be involved in—while they felt left out and excluded—only because they missed the clues left hidden. X types often admitted later of a failure to see the hints made. Here's a hint you won't miss: it's better to plan a trip to take your Y type white-water rafting—if that's what he's into (and your goal is bonding)—than go to great lengths to cook a nice, four-course meal with candles at the house.

Communication

In the previous chapter, we noted the differences in how X type and Y type personalities communicate, and these differences were often stylistic. For the purposes of our model, we differentiated them as Xs and Ys—but the fundamental difference is in *how much* they communicate, and this cannot be overstated. Because we have said that for Ys, talk must be functional and purposeful, as opposed to trivial and entertaining, we could presume the conversation of X types to be unnecessary and nonfunctional, but it is neither. It serves the specific function of attaching two individuals who become closer and closer the more they share, in the same way that Y types bond the more they "hang out."

There is more to be gained by spending time with your Y partner, joining them in extracurricular activities of their choice, than trying to engage them in an emotion-laden conversation about how you feel. You should never forget that such sharing pushes Y types away. From the X type's perspective, voluminous sharing means, "I like you, I trust you, I want to get to know you better," and early self-disclosure of a private or personal nature serves to deepen this bond further. But this is not the case with Y types who prefer communication that has been condensed all the way down to sound bites, with no elaboration or details or speculation. Just the facts!

Though Y's self-disclosure would indicate growing closeness, it's seldom done early in the relationship, if at all.

Harry's Small Chip

When Harry "the IT guy" and Suzette were breaking up, they decided to have one more heart-to-heart. She needed closure, and he needed to "listen to *it*" one more time, in the hopes of never having to see her again.

Harry began with, "I never liked talking to you because you always had so much to say and spoke so fast that I couldn't capture everything easily. So rather than let you know I didn't listen to your complaints and have you think I was simply inattentive or stupid, I kept my mouth shut, nodded, and listened. Then after several days, I would return your call hoping that by some miracle you'd calmed down, or at least were on to another topic. What I would find is that you would pick up the conversation exactly where we left off at the uncomfortable spot, where you tried to turn me into a talker or therapist and attempted to get me to analyze a relationship that even you couldn't figure out. Then I'd ask one question that required one short answer. But, no. You'd give me a paragraph for every sentence. Detail after unnecessary detail."

He continued, "If I knew I could come home to a quiet house, I would have come home to you more often, but you'd want to 'talk,' either about stupid, trivial, gossipy things, or heavy, depressing, relationship things. You gave me too much information and too much explanations for everything—and why? You weren't getting a grade for all the extras." This was unusual for a computer scientist. Some have speculated that programmers and IT experts select their careers, in part, as a means of escaping conversation and human interaction. But Harry had a lot on his mind.

Suzette finally got a word in and explained that for problems to be solved, they have to be talked about and analyzed. But she concluded that Harry was more interested in simple girls with no brains who could not think, let alone carry more than one thought at a time. Then she took an unnecessary detour and called Harry's taste in girls "trashy."

When it comes to understanding XY communication, computer analogies work well. There was a time when computers were capable of only one set of computations at a time, but technology was soon able to store and retrieve more data and computations from a smaller chip, and before long we got to where we are today, benefiting from multithreading and hyper-threading technology—able to use multiple processors and conduct many transactions simultaneously or in parallel, with a series of loops and branching.

As we touched on in previous chapters, X types communicate like a multithreaded system capable of opening several files at once, looping and branching from one conversation to the next, never losing their place or the point at which boring banter was abandoned for a more favorable "thread" of conversation. Many Y types seem incapable of, or overwhelmed by, this type of dialogue. Thinking in parallel? Interestingly, computer scientists tell us that you can decrease a computer's performance, *response time*, and quality of response, if you try to run too many operations on a single or serial threading design. Maybe there is something to Y types' careful processing of information after all.

An X Fact

We once thought that women (translate: X types whether male or female) would bring up topics over and over simply because it was helpful for them to be able to vent. Whereas it's true that X types aren't always seeking solutions from their partners—contrary to popular opinion—they're at least hoping to be understood. Several have explained that the lack of resolution that forces them to revisit old topics stems from them feeling their partner isn't even making a serious attempt to consider their plight but instead is dismissive in his or her silence. But what are X types truly interested in resolving? Is it always the stated problem at hand? We'll have to answer these questions a bit later.

Conversational Files

We left Suzette giving her IT boyfriend Harry a piece of her mind. Eventually though, he got in the last word and concluded his discussion by assuring her that she was, in fact, crazy, demanding, and overbearing. At which time Suzette took the opportunity to let him know that for the two weeks he ignored her—because *he* felt threatened or overwhelmed or whatever—she met another guy with whom she had a conversation that lasted six hours, as opposed to the six minutes she often got from Harry. (It took some effort, but I was finally able to convince her that not all men were Y types, and she needed to be on the lookout for X men!)

And what's more, she continued to tell Harry (about her new X man), "I can carry on three and four conversations with him at once. We bounce around from topic to topic like hummingbirds in a flower garden and never get lost like you complained about. Eventually, we discuss everything on the table, and close all our files, conclude all our conversations."

It's always nice to hear clients using the jargon you gave them to describe phenomena as couples communicate, but Harry looked a little hurt by her honesty. She concluded by saying, "Harry, you remember how you would complain about me overwhelming you, how you felt like I was intentionally trying to 'crash' your computer? You don't need to bother any-more. I found someone with a bigger chip!"

Classic Y's

In this chapter, we have covered only the classic Y type personality. As was explained in earlier chapters, I first discov-ered this XY phenomenon about a decade ago. At that time, the vast majority of Ys were showing up consistently low on the communication scale, but the emotional factor was dis-covered years later. Now, though, there has been a seismic shift in the last decade alone; today, some Y communicators have high emotional needs while others are Ys with low emo-tional needs. Here are seven types of Y personalities to help you to classify your partner and better understand him or her.

1. **The Sports Y:** This Y personality uses an obsession with sports—either sporting events or sports on TV—to avoid con-versation and family or bonding time. Needless to say, this is a point of contention for their more X type lovers.

2. **Outdoor Y's:** These types love outdoor activity and become irritable if they have to stay indoors for too long. There is a noticeable shift in mood once the outdoors are embarked upon, where their favorite means to bond by sharing in an

activity can be enjoyed. This is a point of contention and con-flict for many couples and Ys should take painstaking effort to be matched with someone who loves the "outdoors" as much as they do.

3. **Social Y's:** Often confused for X types when first observed in social settings, these are the mates who have an obligation to spend quality time with their buddies or girlfriends, but they often do so to the point that it affects the relationship. They become animated and talkative in ways that their partners at home never see. Social Ys are often mistaken for communi-cative X types, but their communication is social in nature, rather than relational, which is why they tend to shut down with their partners at home.

4. **Self-Absorbed Y's:** Self-absorbed Ys can sometimes be confused with Social Ys. But here's how you can tell them apart. Social Ys prefer an audience, whereas self-absorbed Ys are often satisfied with one listener . . . You! He or she can drone on and on about topics of their own interest. Try and interject with another topic of your own and you'll soon discover this was not a conversation but his soliloquy. Your Y partner has little interest in your stories . . . unless you can find a way to make it about him.

5. **Old Media Y's:** They preoccupy themselves with TV shows, though not necessarily sports, as well as games such as X-Box, Nintendo, Wii, but also can spend an inordinate number of hours on the computer (not including social networking).

6. **Social Media Y's:** They spend time on social networks and visiting dating sites and playing with the latest creation on the Internet. In fact, President Obama is said to have collaborated with Facebook executives over the role they would play in the first election, which he subsequently won. We'll talk more about him a little later in book II, and whether we can predict (analyze) his personality by studying his politics.

7. **Hobby Y's:** These Ys engage in some hobby that requires the minimum of interaction or conversation with significant others. Fascination or preoccupation with the latest gadget falls into this category, as do memberships in groups requiring little or no interaction. Some men take up gardening or tinkering while women can do crochet or solitaire, Sudoku or read several novels.

8. **Pre-Occupied Y's:** These get the lion's share of complaints filed against them by their X type partners. The criticisms are generally over the fact that they fail to engage conversation-

ally with their partners, often ignoring questions, failing to listen attentively or make eye contact, and always seeming as if they're in deep thought—their own thoughts and self-interests—leaving partners feeling neglected and slighted.

9. **Career Y's:** Ys as you might have guessed, use their careers to shield themselves from interacting with their partner or family at home. They work very hard, put in a lot of hours and seem very diligent (which are all indisputable Y traits anyway). But, their bottom line is, avoidance and that, they've gotten it down to a science.

Chapter 8

XY Differences

Timelines and Commitment

*B*ecky waited for one year for a commitment. During that time, she was faithful and true. She cooked his food, washed his clothes, and allowed him to stay at her house for free. She hoped he would get over his ex-girlfriend of five years and commit to her, but a commitment never came. She was caught in what I call the *Developmental Trap*. Y types have a good idea of when they could conceivably settle down, and until then, anyone caught in their path, their trap, falls prey to timing. Becky met Andre when she was just 19. He was 21 and considered himself too young for marriage. He in fact explained, after taking the test, that he didn't see himself getting married before he was 30 because no one in his family married young, and he had no intention of being the first. He wasn't cheating on her, so she felt she couldn't leave him, but he wasn't "mature" enough to make a serious commitment either. She was in love with him but was now caught in his trap.

So what exactly were Andre's intentions for Becky then? Was she one in a string of romances taking turns on Andre's musical chair of love? Where whoever was fortunate enough to be sitting on the chair last—when he hit his predetermined year for marriage—would become the lucky girl?

When couples were interviewed, it was clear that X types were following their hearts, whereas Y types were following their heads and their timing. Developmentally, Y types seemed ready somewhat later for long-term commitment than their X type partners. The issue came up so often in interviews that I cautioned younger women to always ask questions that would give them a sense of when their Y partner might be ready to settle down. If this is your predicament, you can make an informed choice as to whether at age 21, for example, you would want to be someone's pillow for the 9 years that it might take them to get to their pre-set age 30, or if you're what they really want. Unfortunately, some Y types never seem to grow up, never mature enough, to get positioned for commitment, marriage, and family by the time their X types are ready.

At least that was the predicament Ruby found herself in with Jack. When they met, they were both 28. Jack didn't tell her that he didn't want children or to be married before 35. He admitted to us at the Institute that he knew all along but didn't want to scare her off. He loved her and could see himself spending the rest of his life with her, but time and courage got away from him, and now at 43 she resented him for the wasted years and the fact that she would probably never have children of her own without medical risks. She explained that she had invested so many of the best years of her life, her youth, and her childbearing years, that it was now pointless to leave, even though she no longer loved him the way she had before.

Hint: What you need to know is exactly at what age your Y partner believes he or she should get married. What you may be used to asking, however, is, "So, where do you see yourself in 5 or 10 years?" If he assumes you're asking about his career instead of simply answering the relationship question you asked, then you probably don't have all the information you need to know. A better question to ask, however, is, "Relationally, where do you see yourself at 25, 30, or 35?" The typical Y partner has a predetermined date or age for marriage that would almost never match what you would expect or want—especially if you're a mixed (XY) couple. Many Ys tend to overshoot and drag you along, past the age you expected, like a pilot who can overrun a runway in bad weather.

The developmental trap is pertinent not only to teenagers or twenty-somethings but also to divorcees as well.

Ruben and Mary had dated for four years. He knew that his Y type partner had been married twice before, but so had he. It never occurred to him to ask about her "secret" rule that she would never marry three times. Arbitrary? Perhaps. But it was her rule, and he could have been spared the four years he spent with her if he had only known about it.

Lisa, 45, dated a 52-year-old man who had never had children. She figured that at his age, he wouldn't be expecting from her the one thing she couldn't give anymore—children. Maybe she shouldn't have assumed. Their relationship ended when he brought up the issue of wanting children and she gently pointed out that he would be 70 at his first child's high school graduation.

You versus Them

There are a considerable number of differences between you and your Y type lover. Here are some of them. They are written for the X type reader since X types are more often the personality types to complain about differences:

- You communicate explicitly, plainly, and with elaboration. Your Y partner relies on inferences, communicating *im*plicitly and in summaries or small snatches. What you have to say is said with flair, in 3D, and (high definition) with all of the detail that befits a good story. Ys are not interested in story details, especially common, everyday stories, and will likely cut you off, tune you out, or walk away from you in mid-sentence.

- To your Y partner, the content of a conversation matters, but not to you. And if a story was good the first time you heard it, it will be even better the second and third time around when *you* tell it. But function is the order of the day for your Y lover, and if what you're saying serves no purpose, then it's as good as gossip and need not be told. Because talking *is* bonding for X types, Xs are often left feeling unfulfilled and lonely in their own homes and in their relationships with an unresponsive mate. Sociologists and psychologists at our institute have calculated that you use at least twice as many words as your Y type partner to communicate the same information. This helps to explain why you are on the unlimited phone plan, with unlimited talk and text, while he's on the most limited plan and can still have roll-over minutes at the end of every month.

- You are more likely to be an emotional creature, which, contrary to what your partner believes, does not mean you are needy, dependent, or overly sensitive. Rather, you are sympathetic, warm, and caring. You're not afraid, as your partner is, to show your emotions and vulnerabilities. You'll ask for a hug when you need one, express your love to him or her when you feel it, and you expect the same in return. But classic Ys do not share your need to share and show, and you will certainly not see the reciprocation in communication or emotion. In fact, Y types have often been described as living in a rhetorical world. When asked why they won't answer questions you've asked them, the frequent answer is, "I didn't know that needed an answer. I thought it was a rhetorical question."

- As an X type individual, you believe in accountability (i.e. consideration for the person you're dating or married to). You would never conceive of getting home an hour or two late without calling, nor would you take a plane trip somewhere without saying you arrived safely. But to your partner, this accountability and consideration is all quite unnecessary communication. This isn't as bad as it sounds. You just need to know and understand the type of priority Ys will put on sharing information. If your Y type was wounded or had a serious accident along the way, rest assured, you would get a short and probably unemotional account of what happened. No call

151

means everything is fine, and like other Xs before you, you can probably adjust to the communication shortfall.

- If you're an emotional X, you believe that you're in a relationship to be of some support to your partner emotionally and will run to his side in a time of crisis—but lace up your Converse—because he will likely be running *away* from you. You are not to see yourself as an emotional freak when this occurs. You just didn't know that Y types prefer to be alone in a crisis, to handle their problems in solitude and silence, and this might include no touching, no hugging, no condolences, no closeness, no suggestions, and no questions. Just respectful silence and space. Lots of space. You can do this!

- This will all be covered in greater detail in later chapters, but your view on sex is as diametrically opposed to your Y type partner's view as the North Pole is from the South. Sex will bond you to your lover, but this act doesn't have quite the same "stickiness" with him or her. As long as you remember that to Ys, sex is an activity and not an ultimate expression of love and affection, you will be OK. Do not get sucked into the emotion of it. Y types will stay with someone for good sex like they will hold on to a golf buddy who provides them with a free pass to the country club so they can get in without a membership fee.

- Your need for verbal reinforcement is unfortunate, if you plan to spend the rest of your life with someone who doesn't believe in anything verbal or anything that requires verbal interaction, such as commitments, conflict resolution, planning, or sharing. When Chris Rock—actor/comedian—said in one of his excellent HBO specials years ago that "women will settle down and get married, but men 'surrender,'" he was really referring to Y type men (and women), and not to you Xs.

- Who will be the one worrying about the relationship, the family, the children, and the impact of the economy? You will. One X type woman had to leave home to go to her Y partner's parent's home to take care of *his* father who had fallen ill. Her husband didn't even know about it, and when he did, he didn't care nor did he show any appreciation. As a result, many X types we interviewed described their husbands and wives as inconsiderate, selfish, self-serving, and arrogant.

- About the arrogance. It stems in part from the fact that your need for communication and emotional support often leads them to believe that you need them more than they need you. It wouldn't matter if they were unemployed and disabled; you would still—as the sole provider—be considered the *needy* one.

- Do not make promises that you're either unwilling or unable to keep. Remember what we said earlier in the book. Actions speak louder than words to your Y mates, but it's just the opposite for you. So what you *say* will be treated like a promise made before God, and you will be held to it.

- Many X types complained that their Y partners were unfair in that they would expect certain courtesies of their X partners but would not do the same in return. We talked about Y types' lack of accountability, but there is also an enormous problem with reciprocation (we will visit this concept again later), so don't you think for a moment about being 15 minutes late and coming home to an understanding lover. There is no two-way street in an XY relationship, but there is a highway. That's correct. It's their way, or, you guessed it, *you* could take the highway.

- You will certainly be the one adapting, changing, assimilating, and conforming to make this relationship work, because Xs have reported consistently that their partners will not. This is not the best kept secret. Go right now and ask your partner what his or her views are on this. Even when interviewed as a couple in front of colleagues and me, there hasn't been much subtlety or secrecy in the answers provided.

- Who makes the better parent? Particularly with men, it would seem that Y type men are not as paternal and caring as X men, but there may be some genetic reasons for this. We can go into this in more depth when discussing hormones and genetics in chapter 12.

- Many Y types have been described as detached and aloof with regard to their ability or inability to bond like X types do, whether male or female. But this, too, we will cover later in greater depth. I promise.

Some Final Impressions from X Type Mates

I asked the X types we interviewed to each give me one word that describes their partner. Some of them used one word, while others—in true X style—gave one word followed by an elaboration, but this is the gist of what they felt:

Strong; not very touchy-feely; unemotional; impassionate; boring; mysterious; thoughtless; inconsistent; cold or cold-blooded; disconnected; focused; hardworking; not good multitaskers; non-communicative but reliable; good at task completion; not distractible; so organized; pragmatic; cool under pressure; good employees; good listeners (but you'll never know); and complex.

The Christmas Date

During the Christmas season of 2011, a man ran an advertisement explaining that he was looking for a date for Christmas. But here was the catch: he was not looking for a girlfriend or a wife. This was not the plea of a lonely man needing a companion. Ads like those appear every day. This one was different.

The man was specific in his need for a *Christmas companion* only. The relationship would end immediately and abruptly after the Christmas season. No further promises made, no questions asked. This man didn't even consider the possibility that he might actually like the woman who agreed to this. Or *worse*—he might fall in love. This was clearly an unusual request. But the only thing to top it was the number of women who responded to this ad…quite a large number. Who were these women?

Naturally, this story begged for my analysis. Was the man a Y type personality? More than likely. And the women? It would depend on their individual goals and expectations. I actually applaud this man's honesty. Y types almost always know their goals for relationships. They know if their attraction for you is only skin deep and temporary. Most do not state their intentions at the start, but some do. As for these women, the Y types among them would appreciate the pragmatic approach and may even be OK with a temporary Christmas status. The Xs who contacted this guy would hope that the few weeks they spend with him would be enough to change his mind. Time and effort would open his eyes, and what he had clearly stated as temporary, he would soon realize he desperately needed and wanted to keep.

Chapter 9

Y Type Women

With regard to relational personality, as you know, personal observations and speculative conclusions are unreliable. Unless you can speak to individuals in person and ask specific test questions subtly, observing someone from a distance yields very little reliable information. And when the distance between observer and the observed is great, scientists refer to this data as parasocial. This would mean you can only make assumptions about someone—such as celebrities you've never met in person—and must rely on media reports to make personality judgments. Yet, many of us make lifetime decisions to be with someone with little more than parasocial information about them.

In spite of this fact, we couldn't help speculating about whether several of our political power couples such as Bill and Hillary Clinton and the Bushes (senior) were comprised of Y type women, known for pushing their partners to succeed. But if one of those Y type women is saddled with an X type man, there is the typical XY conflict, along with complaints from the "X", of a partner's coldness, neglect or lack of intimacy, which often can lead to what we call "type" infidelity.

In our use of letters to describe the personality types of a *couple*, it's important to remember that the first letter or letters in a match configuration refers to the female in the relationship, and the second letters to the male. A designation describing a mixed couple as YX indicates that the female is a classic Y (Y communicator as well as an unemotional Y). Keep in mind that according to XY theory, the letters represent levels of need. An X communicator is an X type because he or she has a high need for communication, while a Y type has a considerably lower need for communication. The typical YX couple would have met in high school. She might have been a cheerleader, and he might have been the quarterback of the football team or the center on the basketball team. Or they could have met in college or on the job, where at first glance he would have been attracted to her poise, her independence, her self-confidence, and her quiet strength. She would have been attracted to his kindness; his compassion; his ability to make her laugh; and his easy-going, flexible approach to life. These would have made his claims to want to please her seem convincing.

On second glance, he would have been attracted to her intelligence, her clarity about who she was and what she wanted out of life—certainly what she wanted in a partner. She might have been on her way to medical school, engineering, or politics. She would most likely be a career woman. If she wanted to study law, and if, as future politicians, they met in law school, he would have thought about his political aspirations and remembered that behind a successful man is a strong woman who understands the sacrifices that would be required.

I would agree that behind or beside many extremely successful men are strong, Y type women. And why do I say that? It isn't that X type women are not ambitious, successful, or supportive. In fact, the X type woman is more likely to abandon her interests to support her partner with his goals and dreams. X types are also more likely to give up their own pursuits of a high-powered career to raise a family or care for the home. The difference lies in whether the support they offer, allows for closeness, togetherness and bonding. Even in working together, bonding is possible for the X. The problem arises with the solo projects that take the Y partner away from family.

What's more, X type women tend to influence their husbands in ways that lead them to put in less time on the job in order to spend more time at home. To the contrary, the Y female is more tolerant of the time her partner needs to be away, because she does not need to have the same level of closeness that her X counterparts would.

The X type woman is more likely to have this type of argument with her frustrated Y: "We've had this conversation before, and I've told you every time: We don't need this big house. For all I care, we can go right back to the 900-square-foot apartment we started with when we first got married. I think we were happier then. Why would I want this big house? There's only more to clean—and you're not here to help me anyway because you're too busy working extra hours *away* from home—so we can keep this big house that I clean by myself. I don't think this is a better deal for me. It's not a better deal for your children, who can't even remember what their father looks like! If I could have my way, you would quit that job today. You would go back to the last job you had that allowed you to get home—before the sun went down—so you could play with your children. We could have dinner again as a family. That's what I'd want, if you asked me."

The Y partner would typically respond by saying something along these lines: "I don't get why you're always nagging. I work 60 hours a week so we can have this roof over our heads. This 3500-square-foot house didn't build itself. Working extra hours to get that promotion is how this all got here. Do you think I worked this hard when I was single? I didn't. I spent Friday evening drinking with the boys. I'm obviously not doing this for my ego."

This conversation is played over and over in homes where the couple is in a mixed XY relationship and the husband is a Y type. But what happens when the female in the relationship is the Y?

The answer to this is completely dependent on the needs and goals of the individual. The man seeking to be a partner in a power couple should probably find himself a Y type female. If you were sure that you wanted to go for partner at your law firm, an executive position at your Fortune 500 company, or some other job that takes you away from home for several days at a time—and you wanted a woman who would support you and push you to be all that you could be and never nag you about it and never complain about the time that you spend away from family to accomplish these goals—then, you might consider seeking a Y type female for a partner. Remember, though, that these are generalizations, and although personality types can predict behavior, they really are predicting only the *probability* that certain behaviors will be exhibited by certain personality types, in certain situations.

Also, remember that as with everything else in life, where there are pros, there are cons. Because this book was written during the worst recession experienced worldwide, many X type men married to Y type women had wives who were the epitome of support and strength prior to the recession—but who were anything but, once the crisis began. Before the threat to the family's security, Y types who were building up their husbands and helping by taking up the slack domestically with chores and children to allow him the extra time he needed to put in extra at work often became nagging, forceful drill sergeants once their husbands lost their jobs.

One husband complained at the Research Institute that his wife would quiz him at the end of every day when she got home from work. She needed to ascertain that he spent his time every single day filling out new job applications, and she never relented for the 18 months that he was out of work. It took him longer than it should have to get another job because of her stipulations. He was not to accept any job that would lower their standard of living in any way. This meant the job had to pay him as much as before or more. Second, the job had to pay him more than she made because she would "feel weird to be with a man who made less than she did." He felt that he no longer recognized this woman who showed a side of her personality that he had never seen in their 25 years of marriage, and it took the worst recession in his lifetime to reveal it.

Y type women we interviewed admitted they had been called gold-diggers before. This derogatory term is used to describe women whose sole purpose for pursuing a specific partner is for monetary gain and financial security. Love and even compatibility were secondary or unimportant. In this regard, many goal-oriented Y type women felt misunderstood, and the more I listened to their heartfelt stories, the more I thought I understood the misunderstanding.

Their *goal* orientation that drove their behavior was often mistaken for *gold*-driven motivation. But there are a few other reasons their intentions might be misconstrued. Like their Y male counterparts, marriage for the Y type woman is a contract more than it is a commitment. The contractual obligations their partner subscribed to are interpreted as his promising to "be a [stereotypical] man," which included a promise to provide for her and the family—and when that promise is broken, when her partner is unable to stay employed or fails to seek compa-rable reemployment, it compromises his ability to ensure that the family maintains its standard of living. It creates a major rift in the relationship and mars or taints his image as a man in her eyes. Some women admitted they knew it was unfair to their X type men, but they couldn't help but feel the way they did and couldn't explain why.

Once in the privacy of my office, out of the earshot of their X type partners, Y type women felt free to really express how they felt, and it wasn't very complimentary. For some, it was almost as if love flew out the window on the wings of the hundred dollar bills these men could no longer bring home.

That is, if you weren't aware that a relationship for a Y type resembles a business partnership, while for Xs the relationship is more about emotionality and love; if you only lend a superficial ear to their explanations. But if you take the time to listen to the true motivation behind their emotion-charged defense, you learn that many of them were not in it for the gold. They were in it to be part of a partnership that was prosperous and progressive. The bottom line for Y type women is that a partner should add to their lives and not subtract from it. It is interesting to note that at the end of those very relationships, X types claimed that they gave more than they received in the relationship and eventually left feeling used. Make no mistake, Y couples are held together by a bond that is very different from the type of bond that an X type woman has with her X mate.

The Y Trap

By now you know that we are matched with each other according to our need for communication *along* with our need for intimacy. One client, Brian, told us of a woman he met who talked a lot at the beginning of his relationship, in their first few weeks after meeting. She would text him all the time, call him often, tell him how special he was and, eventually, how much she loved him and would do anything to be with him. When he first told me about her, knowing he had an XX type of personality, I excitedly gave him the green light. But within three months, the relationship had become a nightmare. This was early in our XY testing at the Institute when communication needs as a factor was everything, and the emotional needs were thought to be secondary in importance. But she had no shortage of intimacy or emotional expression, so how had this gone so wrong?

I begged him to get her in for XY testing. He succeeded after two months, and her reluctance gave me my first clue about what might have gone wrong. Brian was a high X communicator and an individual with equally high intimacy needs. To see these two together, at least between their fights, they couldn't get enough of each other; they were so touchy-feely. But let's take a look at those personality types again.

Relationship Needs

XX	X-Communicator & Emotional-X
XY	X-Communicator & (Un)Emotional-Y
YY	Y-Communicator & (Un)Emotional Y
YX	Y-Communicator & Emotional X

She talked a lot and was very intimate. But here is the danger in not testing a prospect before getting into a relationship or taking a careful sample of communication. We'd talked to him about the usefulness of using the "text test." The overwhelming majority of Y communicators tends to text less and use shorter texts. This would be your first clue, especially in the first three months of the relationship, which some refer to as the honeymoon period. I asked him if he'd kept his text messages from the first two months. The romantic sap that Brian was, I had no doubt that he'd erased nothing. When we took a look at the texts, they were *all* of an emotional or intimate nature. They had both exchanged texts by week two of the relationship. One of his texts said, "I think I'm falling in love with you."

Hers said, "Really? Oh, my gosh! I was just about to say that!"

Then, he said, "But I told you first."

And she said, "Yes, and it makes me feel so close to you. Like this was meant to be."

This went on for weeks. But our prying revealed one important finding. There were *no posts* of a casual or social nature. No small talk from her. No, "How was your day today?" Absolutely no small talk. This girlfriend of his was a pro at what is called "*emoting*"! This is the practice of or ability to share emotions freely, to communicate one's feelings. This would qualify her as an emotional X. A high emotional X, according to the test. But her score in the area of casual communication, which by design excludes emoting as a type of communication, showed that she had a communication need that fell in the low Y range.

This is the first time we've needed to *clarify* that the first X in the personality configuration of an individual, refers specifically to "social" conversation. But for X types, social, everyday conversation has a relationship implication. Remember, we said earlier that one error some of us have made is to assume that the personality we see exhibited in a *social* setting is the true and lasting personality? This is very often misleading because in certain social settings, we are more likely to exhibit our social personality, which is often the opposite of how we function relationally. Following is the best example of that:

A YX woman and an XX man
(A mixed couple in the area of social conversation.)

About three months into the relationship, just when the hormones had declined, and emoting (sharing feelings) had done its job (to bond the pair), Brian discovered that his girl seemed to show a stark disinterest in his daily life, goals, and dreams, or small talk. At that point, he did not know that Y types, generally disinterested in their partner's dreams, because of their disaster for the intangible, prefer to focus on the destination and not on the journey along the way. In fact, a two-hour cab ride through the city gave him the first clue of their XY difference, when he could not woo her to join him in any of his conversations as she had very little to say.

But the trap was already set. A Y trap, to be exact. Unlike most traps, this one is not intentionally set by any one partner—yet it affects and afflicts them both. At the Institute, we quickly pointed out the problem and enrolled the couple in our XY Workshop because they expressed a desire to stay together. Brian was taught to adjust his expectations as well as his communicative needs. His girlfriend, who is now his fiancée, will now at the end of the day ask him how his day was and be intentionally interactive whenever they get together.

At the risk of overstating this, let me say that a Y type woman is any woman with even one Y in her personality configuration. Even if she is a Y communicator and an emotional X, the parts of her personality that are high X will never be high enough to compensate for her Y-ness—or help her X type mate to feel totally complete and satisfied. Any X type man who intentionally dates a Y type woman must be prepared to make considerable adjustments because it isn't in the nature or personality of the Y type female (or male) to be the one who makes the majority of the changes or compromise.

Suddenly

It was three days before Christmas, and Kim was sitting at home with her fiancé, Sean, and her best friend at the dining table. They were having a casual conversation (or so he thought) before the topic swung to relationships; His girl-friend, Kim's relationship! (Kim was given the XY Personality test and had a low need for communication.) Kim's best friend wanted her to explore her relationship with her fiancé sitting at the table. To her credit, Kim tried to worm her way out of it, but her best friend missed the cue and barreled on. Her boyfriend couldn't look more confused. As far as he knew, they had no major issues. An occasional argument, maybe, but she never mentioned any major concerns.

"You know you're unhappy," her friend said. "Let's talk about your relationship with your husband-to-be, "Sean."

Kim repeated with a raised voice, "I don't want to talk about my relationship."

By this time, even Sean wanted to know what was on her mind and concluded that she must have been complaining behind his back instead of dealing with the issues directly with him, and privately. But this was not Kim's style. As a Y communicator, she liked to sweep personal conflict under the rug and not discuss it with her partner. Not so with her best friend Monica, a high X communicator, who couldn't even take a cue to shut up after her friend indicated that she didn't want to deal with what she had told her in confidence. The fact is, Xs often gossip because bonding occurs even when the content of a conversation is negative, or at times unpleasant.

Sean had always wondered how Monica and Kim ever became such close friends. He was probably confused by the fact that his fiancé was not a talker, but her best friend was. (He was allowing his mind to wander on the past as his way of avoiding the obvious tension in the room.) He had heard the story of their first meeting several times from the best friend— but only once from his own fiancé. They had met at the community hospital years ago in the pediatric unit. Ironically, they had both given birth to two premature babies and felt it was such serendipity that led them to each other that they made the decision, then, to raise their children together as friends, as much as they could. But how did it last if the mothers were so different? Sean slowly drifted back to the present.

At some point, Kim's face had become tighter, more serious. Sean claimed that he'd always had difficulty "reading" her. He couldn't tell when he did something wrong. He couldn't tell when he upset her or when she was unhappy. She didn't complain much. She certainly wasn't a nag. If something was wrong, she would bring it up once—quietly—using as few words as possible, and never mention it again, even if the problem had not been remedied. As far as he was concerned, they didn't have an ideal relationship, but it wasn't bad, and they never had serious fights. In this area, he was quite the opposite. If something bothered him, he would tell her right away, and often—in fact, as often as it took to allow him to feel that she understood what was wrong. But they didn't both need to handle their differences in such a dramatic way, so Sean really appreciated her calm disposition.

Kim had a little boy from a previous relationship, so Sean played step-dad to him, and the two became very close. From the outside, no casual observer could tell he was not the biological father. They played together, he read his bedtime stories to him, and he gave the boy his baths before putting him to bed.

When Kim's son was two, he suffered from coughing fits at night. He would be awakened by convulsions from acid reflux that plagued him from birth. Kim almost never heard the first signs of these fits. She slept like a log. By the time she did awake, her fiancé was already holding the little boy and comforting him. Sean even succeeded in learning to slide out of the bed so as not to disturb Kim, so with time she learned to trust his emerging parenting skills and was able to sleep on.

But today was not about his relationship with that child. It wasn't about whether he was a better parent to her son than the biological father was, who was "missing in action" and hadn't been seen in a year. In fact, Sean had no idea what today was about and why Kim's best friend needed to come to the house to act as mediator. So it came as a surprise when Kim's best friend finally said, "Look you two, I know what's going on. Let's talk about the relationship." Then she turned to Kim, "You love Sean, don't you?"

As cool as a cucumber, Kim said, "I don't think so. Not anymore!"

"What? What do you mean?" Sean asked, finally perking up.

"But I don't," Kim insisted, coldly.

When Sean looked at Kim's friend for answers, she seemed more shocked than he. She looked as though she wished she had never brought it up. But she couldn't back out now. She had started it and had to see it through. Somewhat. Sean was devastated and embarrassed. He hadn't seen this coming and couldn't understand why someone—anyone— would spring something like this so suddenly. So publicly. As a high X communicator on the XY scale, he would never have done that. But in the same vein, because of his X type personality his heart was now pushing him to probe further while his head was telling him to leave it alone. If he were a Y type like his wife-to-be, he would have gotten up to save himself from further pain and embarrassment. But he wasn't, and so he didn't. It is not the X way. It wasn't his personality.

He pushed her again with his words, "So you don't love me?"

She said, "No. I don't. I mean, I'm not sure. I don't think so."

And then her best friend chimed in, "You don't love him?" (Kim didn't answer her.) Her friend asked again, "Why don't you love him?"

She said, "Because I don't, I don't. Look, he doesn't have any more money."

Her friend said, "Please tell me this is not about money. You don't love him anymore because his money ran out?" (Obviously she had not been told enough to put the pieces together herself.)

And as stereotypically honest as Y types tend to be, because they often don't really care sometimes about subtlety, Kim said, "Yeah, that's it exactly. He doesn't have any more money. When I look at him and at us as a couple, I just don't see any light at the end of the financial tunnel. I know that he's had financial problems before, and I know he's been able to recover, but from this one, I don't think so."

What made this story so strange was that this horrendous exposé about her relationship with Sean—her falling out of love for financial reasons—was all discussed at the kitchen table right in front of Sean, who just sat there dumbfounded. Paralyzed, perhaps, but mortified certainly.

Kim's friend uncomfortably shuffled a bit and then got up and got her handbag and left. Sean got up from the table and slipped out the door and called me on his cell. I had known Sean for some time, and I happen to know he made good money but bad investments; he was a very enterprising man who did his best to start a few businesses. Some went well while others went belly up, and Kim stood by his side. In fact, she stood by his side so hard that several members of her family and friends asked her if she didn't think she was doing too much. "You're giving more than your 100 percent. You're doing the work of three women. You're keeping the house together, raising your son, and helping him with his businesses. When he has to fly out of the country to take care of those businesses, you're left raising your kid alone and managing the home affairs for months at a time, without him. Why are you doing all this?" her friends asked.

She never complained. She and Sean were the consummate power couple, and she, the consummate Y type woman. But also, like Y type women, when the dam breaks, it does so suddenly and irreparably. Like their male counterparts, Y type women do not give warning of impending relational doom. With Ys, you're more likely to come home and find the house cleaned out and your Y type wife gone without a hint of marital problems. Much more so than you would with X type females. The gold-digger motif often isn't well earned by Y type women. At least it's not *honestly* earned by the Ys, but the reason it is given is easily understood.

It's important to keep in mind that every personality type has its pros and cons. The drama that Y type men complain about in women they date or with their X wives at home, is more typical of emotional X type women. High emotional scores mean a partner who is prone to more worry, sensitivity, anxiety, and higher need for your attention, affection and emotional support. There will be careers you might embark on that would exacerbate and highlight the downside of her personality. Careers that take you away from home—such as those of truck drivers, police officers, firemen, the armed forces, intelligence agencies, law, medicine, executive positions in corporations—are all liabilities because of the distance and the time they take from the relationship. If you're both X types, then you'll both equally suffer in this way and both collaborate to come up with plans to reduce the effects. But if you're in a mixed relationship, you, the Y type, will seem lacking in empathy for the needs and stated concerns of your partner.

On the other hand, partners of Xs can expect nurturing, attention, and emotional support at the level of their need if both partners are on the same level on the XY scale. If you're a Y type partner and you choose another Y type partner, you reduce the probability for having emotional outbursts or the conflict-style loop, where your partner makes demands and you withdraw to avoid the hostile emotional exchange, after which your withdrawal triggers a reaction from your partner which forces you to withdraw even more. It certainly is a trade off, but you should be guided in your choice by your future goals, current needs, and experience with the different personality types in your past. Instead of viewing the Y type female as a gold-digger, keep in mind that she might turn out to be a gold mine; Ys are better at supporting practical goals that can improve the couple's or family's status, while X type females will more likely allow you to pursue the artist's dream with no guarantee of success simply because it makes you happy and doesn't take you away from home for too long.

Y + Y =?

After all we've learned, shouldn't Ys just date Y types? I found it interesting that I have never been asked this question by an X type. Never once in all my years of researching this theory, have I been asked by an X, "Would I be better off if I ended this relationship and went with someone who has my personality type?" Why is it that an X would never ask that but Ys often do? Often. I had to think about this carefully. But I suppose that's the whole point of this theory and the whole point of the book. If I could catch someone before they got into a relationship and advise them to find their personality type and seek out only people who were of their type, they would have a much better chance at happiness than those who went into it with the typical blindfold.

Your Dance with Chance

When I shared this theory with a close friend's boyfriend who was in his 20s, he said to me, "What would you have given to be my age and to know what you know right now about XY theory?"

I laughed and said, "Hey, I'm not that old, you know. And by the way, I did know about XY theory over ten years ago, but I fought it and refused to accept the theory, let alone change my dating pattern because of it." I needed those 10-plus years, though, of experimenting, observing, and interviewing hundreds of others to be able to codify this theory so I could share it with you and others in a systematic and helpful way.

I know now that we have two personalities. One for non-intimate social gatherings, and the other to be expressed the moment our brain realizes that this person we might have kept as a platonic friend for years is now about to be seriously considered for a change of status. Then the dangerous, and often destructive, test begins. Not the XY Personality test, but the test of whether we would be willing to dance with chance.

But now to answer the question my friend's boyfriend asked earlier that I tried to skirt around: I would give anything to get back 10 years of my life if I could date according to XY theory. Instead, during the past decade, I hit my head on a lot of walls, got my heart broken more times than necessary, and yes, to use the old cliché, "If I only knew back then what I know now!"

But what would her boyfriend do now, after three hours of my explaining all this to him? I also tested him, and he was a low level Y in both communication and emotions. He seemed amazed at first that his girlfriend—who was tested previously and received high scores in both communication and emotion—fought with him a lot, knew what he now knew, and still wanted to be with him. Then he pulled me into the kitchen so his girlfriend—who had come over to the house to visit that day—would not hear him, as he asked, "So do you think that if I broke it off with my girlfriend, I would be happier with a Y type like I am?" I said, "Yes, in some ways you would be."

I didn't go into further detail with him. But I will with you. It would be easier for Y types to be together when it comes to conflict resolution. They would both sweep problems under the rug and process them quietly and individually. Remember what Dr. Gottman found? Couples who avoided verbalizing areas of conflict, in that they did not talk about the problem continuously and refused to harp on the topic, were often happily married for decades and did just fine. We said this was because voicing highly emotionally charged criticisms are often detrimental to the relationship. He is not alone in thinking this way. In fact, several books now contend that it's a myth that happily married couples are conflict free.

Research supports that happily married couples have conflict, as do all couples, but they handle it in *the same way*. So if they're both extreme Ys, neither of them would be extremely affectionate and neither of them would expect an inordinate amount of emotional support or attention from the other. They would feel that the arrangement was nice. Comfortable. They would also pretty much have "silent night" every night in their home and not just at Christmas time, unless they decided to strike up a conversation on one of their many or few topics of self-interest. Then they would talk about that for as long as they felt they needed to, maybe bond a little, and then go to bed. There would probably be no pillow talk. They wouldn't expect texts and phone calls during the day, disturbing them from their important work, since Ys are more likely to obsess about their careers, sometimes to the dismay of their X type partners, who think that they put work ahead of family. So the YY couples could have a lot going for them.

But they also have quite a few pitfalls.

Pitfall #1: A Mixed-match. Before running away from his X type partner, a Y type has to be sure that he's focusing on the whole picture. He has to be sure that he understands the difference between an Extreme relationship and an Inverted relationship. In Extreme relationships, the X type person has an XX personality. Remember we talked about the two designations of the classic XX type—a high need for communication, and high secondary needs such as attention, affection, affirmation, and so forth...needs that contribute to feelings of intimacy. High secondary needs and high communication needs would give you an XX type personality. The opposite is true of the classic YY: he has a low need for affection, attention, attachment, and verbal expressions of emotion, and certainly has no need for trivialized, nonfunctional social conversation. No need for chit-chat, although this is not to say that your Y type partner won't chit-chat. They may try to please the X type partner, but they don't *need* it like their partner does.

Xs bond by chit-chatting, and that's the reason very often their topics seem shallow to a Y, or trivial, because it's the *act of talking* itself that is the bond for an X type. Not so with Ys. They are more content driven. Functionality is the obsession here. A Y type is likely to leave an X partner and, instead of hooking up with an extreme Y, which is really what he would need, he may find himself in another mixed relationship. What that means is that he may become interested in an individual who has low communication needs, so he rushes right in, thinking that he found someone like himself—only to discover that despite being a Y communicator, she has a high level of secondary needs. She has a YX personality. She, like he, doesn't need social conversation and nonfunctional chit-chat. But the similarities end there. She wants attention and can communicate emotions quite well. She wants the roses. She wants romantic walks on the beach. She would very much enjoy walks in the park, and during these times, she has a high tolerance for talks that build intimacy and that communicate feelings. In addition, she wants him to be home early. She wants to raise children and have a family. Mr. Y is stuck. Déjà vu. He didn't see it coming because he focused only on avoiding a chatty woman. But he is now knee deep in a mixed relationship, if he isn't careful. Even if he were careful to finally find a YY, he is likely to have a huge control issue and the power struggles and rigidity that come with many such relationships.

Pitfall #2: Commitment Problems. This is always a risk with Y partners. Remember, Ys don't measure very high on the attachment scale. They won't really commit to someone they don't feel attached to, so they tend to break up quite easily.

Pitfall #3: Assimilation. Xs adapt and assimilate easily and willingly. But Ys do not. If the scores of both Y partners are equally low, this can mean a premature end to a promising relationship unless one is willing to meet the other halfway. This problem is seen primarily in partners not wanting to learn or participate in each other's hobbies, activities, or interests.

Pitfall #4: Power Struggles and Control Issues. Another risk with two Ys being together is that what you might have is someone who will not adjust to or accommodate the other partner. You might have instead two very stubborn individuals existing in the same space, the same house. The control issues are likely to be enormous and sometimes insurmountable because each feels that he or she knows better than the other. It is unlike an XY relationship, in which the X might say, "OK, you're right"—(and think quietly, "You're wrong, but this is not worth fighting over. I want to save and preserve the relationship.")—Ys don't seem to have the capacity or the will to do that, so a power struggle ensues.

Pitfall #5: Compatibility Issues. This is a critical area for Y types. These partners really need to be very compatible. Although some research out there says that compatibility isn't that important, we've found that to be true only if partners are matched closely in personality and are not in an XY relationship. If you put two individuals together, neither of whom will adjust, compatibility obviously has to be critical, and the

Y couple would want to have as much in common as possible. When an X type falls in love with you, there are several things that would bind them to you, such as the little conversation they would have to eke out of you; the few times that you happen to say that you love them; and then, there's the bonding effect of sex—a lot more bonding for X types than Y types. So at first an X type is not likely to focus on your actions, or lack of, and will probably not leave you because you didn't go out to look for that job after six months of collecting an unemployment check. And if there's a child in the picture, they will take into consideration that they gave birth to your child and have an added responsibility to hang in there, probably forever.

One mixed couple celebrated their 50th anniversary. The wife was an X, the husband a Y. The wife said that in their 50 years together, she had been happy for only one year. Just one year she could say that she had a good relationship, and that was the honeymoon year. From the very first year, she realized she had married an egotistical mate, and it was all downhill from there. But 50 years later, she was celebrating yet another anniversary. That's never going to happen to two Ys. Not gonna happen. Two Ys would look at actions and treat actions as contracts that are kept or broken and require that further action be taken—unless there are strong instrumental reasons to delay action and suspend judgment.

Pitfall #6: And then there is the gold-digger problem again. Yes, unless you are the consummate provider, a consistent breadwinner, you need to be concerned that if things go wrong, your Y type partner might not feel so committed. Ladies, those of you who are Ys, I have to apologize in advance, but this is what Y type women have told me repeatedly. I didn't guess it, nor did I manufacture it. These are your self-reports. When finances become problematic, Ys feel that the bond is weakened because the man is no longer in the provider role that they were attracted to. He has become soft and not the man they once knew. Y type women like "manly" men—men who can change a tire.

I had one woman come in to see me to complain that she was sick of her boyfriend because he wouldn't get out of the car to change a tire, like other men she knew. Of course, I was thinking that considering the neighborhood they lived in, I wouldn't get out to change a tire myself. Even though I know how to do it, I would probably still call AAA or some other roadside service. She explained it was a bit different in her case because her boyfriend did *not know* how to change a tire, and if something happened in the middle of nowhere, why should she be stuck with him? And then she threw in, as an afterthought, that he talked too much.

Chapter 10

What's A Personality?

*T*he fact that you can discover in a few minutes that you're in a relationship where—not just a few mere differences but a major personality difference—can hijack your hopes for the future is as enlightening as it is threatening. If you're not in a relationship that you could describe as "excellent" or "wonderful," you might discover that your partner wasn't just an unreasonable lark but just very different from you. A jerk can change. A jerk you can fix. A dolt you can reason with, sometimes. Fixing your relationship would be within your control. But a personality difference? You're not so sure.

The writing of this chapter coincided with an unplanned dental visit. I broke a tooth while chewing on a bone the size of an atom. The pain of an exposed nerve drove me to the dentist's chair, but instead of my usual dentist treating me, his dental hygienist attended to me. I had promised my dentist a free membership to XYMatchQuest.com[21], the match-making website that utilizes XY theory; however, as he wasn't there that day, I offered the free membership to the hygienist. I always expect individuals to jump at a chance to find out whether they're well-matched with a significant other and even more so if it's free. I explained to her that she could now take her phone out and call her boyfriend of one year, and in less time than it would take the cement to set and dry around the crown on my tooth, they would be able to take the test and see the results simultaneously on their phones.

Still, she hesitated. I assured her that even if she found herself in an XY relationship—which, by the way, is not the easiest match—a 14-week program was available to help them work through it. She seemed relieved. A little. Then asked if she could take the test for both of them, get the results secretly, and show them to him only if the results were good! Luckily, I did have such an option, "The Reluctant Partner Test," created at the Institute, for people like her. She was not the first wanting to take the test by proxy for her partner. What I wasn't prepared for was the request that since she was the one taking the test, she wanted a few minutes of delay before the results could be texted to him, and the option to choose to not have them sent to him at all if she didn't like the results. I had to get on the phone and explain to my Web and App developers that we needed one more change that I happened to think was a useful one.

The idea that she might discover something about her partner that *he* might not want to fix, terrified her. If she had a pain in her lower right abdomen that turned out to be appendicitis, would refusing to go to the hospital to find out whether her appendix had ruptured, change the outcome of her condition in any way? The fact is, if a personality difference was affecting her relationship, her partner would himself also feel that something was wrong. He might not have a label for the problem (an aspect this book helps with), but he would know that the relationship he has with her was not ideal and might still walk away from it.

As you know, our testing and analysis have shown that there are four basic personality types, and each type has various levels of need. What that means is that you have less than a 25 percent chance that your random meeting will result in landing you a soul mate. Whether it's an Internet date or a blind date, to take that chance without each taking the XY Personality test, is like going to Las Vegas for the first time and playing roulette with your last $500 and hoping to get lucky. And for those already in an XY relationship, remember the Scheideweg in chapter 2? The German word we learned, which means the split in the road? All relationships have their ups and downs, but XY relationships have more than their fair share, many of which bring the couple to the split in the road. In this book, *XY theory: The Dangerous Test* and its companion XY Theory Volume II[22], we try to give couples the tools they need to navigate past the crises and sometimes around them. XY couples are notorious for not being able to problem solve because there is often at least one person who does not use a communicative approach to solving the problem. For the techniques from this book to work, though it's ideal, it is not necessary to share them with your partner. However, ignoring the problem won't make it go away.

Other test takers asked about personalities and whether their partners would ever change, so let's talk a little about what constitutes a personality.

The discovery that we have social personalities, or personalities that dictate our behavior in social settings, among platonic friends perhaps at a restaurant or club, is not the dangerous idea that gave rise to the "dangerous test"; rather, it was that research revealed a separate personality whenever romance enters the picture. The date representative—or fictional persona that couples often joke about as the one responsible for giving their significant other an appearance of someone they're not—might be the social personality at work and not a figment of our imaginations. In fact, the word "personality" is taken from the root word "persona," which has a connotation similar to that of the word "mask."

We're all aware that our first date is the time to say nice things about ourselves, our intentions, and most of all, the person sitting across the table from us—our date. What we may not know is that our future will not be with the person who told a white lie to impress, who said you had beautiful blue eyes when you knew your eyes were brown, or who asked if you were a triathlete when your doctor told you that you needed to lose at least 30. No, you're not stuck with the sweet talker who after marriage no longer delivers the sweets, no longer delivers the goods. What you're stuck with is a complete stranger.

You're left wondering how someone as smart as you could have been fooled so easily, so completely. Or how he could be so slick, so devious about his presentation of who he was and what he would do to make you happy if you gave him a chance. Well, as I said before, it wasn't your fault, and very often it's not his either. It's the work of that other personality— that persona that emerges at the mere mention or thought of romantic interest. It is as distinctly different as a nonidentical twin who may bear a resemblance but possesses different tastes, interests, habits, needs, and sensitivity!

That is what to some is scary. But what is dangerous is what lies in the definition of a personality and what that means for you in a relationship. Whether a social relationship or a romantic relationship, each has a distinct personality, and what's viewed as dangerous is the very nature of what a personality is. Personality testing began in the early 1900s (and according to some, a little before). One of the more prominent names among psychologists in the study of personality is Gordon Allport (1897–1967).[23] He believed we had two distinct personalities. One was our childhood personality, while the other was discernible in adulthood. He fully explored the idea of individual behavior being guided by certain traits, and those traits developed and were discernible because of a person's habits. Allport was followed by other trait theorists such as Raymond Cattell and Hans Eysenck and by researchers Robert McCrae and Paul Costa.

However, it wasn't long before modern scientific techniques and research disproved Allport's theory about the separation between childhood traits and adult traits; some studies show that it is possible to look at a three-year-old's temperament and make a reasonable conjecture about how he will behave as an adult. What Allport called functional autonomy, or the belief that adult motives and behavior are a separate (or autonomous) form, and in no way functionally connected to earlier experiences, was grossly incorrect. Allport made important contributions to the field of personality assessment in general, and trait theory in particular, but this was not one of them. In fact, if you are a parent or an older sibling, you can remember who was very talkative or extroverted as a child. Is that person still a talkative extrovert as a teenager or adult? You can also see among your children—who's affectionate and clingy and who would rather not be touched. Has this changed much in adulthood?

There are some biologically based genetic or inherited components to personality that are *difficult to change*. If we say XY theory is one that proposes that we have two dimensions to our personality that can be identified even in early adolescence (and not one personality for childhood and one for adulthood), we're saying that the person you choose to date or inevitably marry, is bringing to the table two distinct dimensions of an adult personality with traits or characteristics that are stable over time and difficult to change. These traits give their inheritors an image of inflexibility. This is the one idea that raises the danger level in the minds of people in a relationship.

Many personality theories and personality tests have been created to assess personality. Some theories depict personalities according to a "type," while others use a "trait" model with characteristics that can be viewed on a continuum. The latter relies heavily on the use of objective tests. Some psychologists feel that "type" personality testing places individuals in a box and lacks flexibility and, at times, accuracy. "Trait" models allow personalities to be considered on a continuum and are more accurate. What "type" testing loses in accuracy, it gains in clarity, while the more accurate "trait" model is more cumbersome, if not complex.

What we've done is combine the best of both worlds by creating a test that can be communicated as a personality type for those who want a quick, basic assessment they can share with others easily. Or, it can be communicated as a more detailed analysis—one that goes into considerably more detail and describes not only the two dimensions measured by the XY Personality test (communication and intimacy), but the levels these dimensions are measured at. This reveals the level of each partner's need.

Traits are habits of behavior that determine how individuals will act in a given situation. But many psychologists (including those of us at The Jacob Research Institute) see these habits as strong, but manageable dispositions and not mandates, which is truly good news. In the social psychology arena, the extroversion/introversion trait is seen as constant and stable from as early as three years old; tests show them to be the same when measured again at age twenty six.[24]

However, if you were hired as a consultant for a firm, or a publicist, or any position that constantly throws you into the public limelight—wouldn't you be able to do well even if you tested as an introvert? Sure. You would do what thousands of other employees around the world who are introverts have ultimately done. You would make the adjustment to your personality, or to the expression of it, so that you could do your job as efficiently as the born extrovert. Wouldn't you? Many Ys adjust for the heavy communication requirements at work and are drained by the time they get home. Well, adjustments can be made for the relationship as well. And though it involves change, it doesn't require a *personality* change.

Because being employed and able to bring a paycheck home to your family or to pay your bills on time is important to you, you will do whatever it takes to "change." In the same way, any boyfriend or husband or wife who values family or the partner they're in relationship with, will make the adjustments necessary to keep what they consider valuable, no matter how strong the personality.

The XY Personality test is a two-dimensional model (communication and intimacy). The test will identify you as having one of four personality types: XX, XY, YX, or YY. In single tests, the first letter represents your designation in the *communication* domain, while the second letter tells you what you need to know about your need for *intimacy*. Because people differ in the degree to which they possess different traits, the letter X in communication or intimacy generally means your personality in that area is on the higher end of the spectrum, and the letter Y, the lower end.

Your personality consists of your unique characteristics showing how you are likely to act or behave in any variety of situations. Having observed these characteristics for more than a decade, it seems to me that those traits that dictate relational behavior remain fairly constant through life *when assessed individually*, and are subject to change only with considerable personal effort, intervention, or some other powerful motivator.

The good news is, whereas your date or significant other can attempt to trick or fool you into thinking they are who they're not, the XY Personality test reveals ahead of time what you would have discovered months or years later. You can now save yourself the agony of what the test shows to be inevitable.

The test was created to assess an individual's relationship personality. We are used to evaluating social personality, how we function and interact in social settings. The best tool to measure this type of personality measures is what psychologists call "The Big Five Factors test." One version developed by McCrae and Costa measures the traits Openness, Conscientiousness, Neuroticism, Extraversion, and Agreeableness.[25] But in relationships, social personality traits fade away, often revealing a relational personality and a person who seems a complete stranger when compared to the social representative. Two relationship factors are required for compatibility and closeness. The first is communication, and the second is a basket of traits that together increase feelings of intimacy in couples. These are the secondary needs. Not secondary in importance, as we noted previously, because individuals who were tested and found to be well matched on the communication scale but mismatched on the intimacy scale were as unhappy as couples with a discrepancy in communication only. A perfect match, or what we refer to on the test as a harmonious match, requires that needs be equally met on the communication scale and on the intimacy scale.

The test is presented in this book in its abbreviated form (it is available on both websites, XYTheory.com and XYMatchQuest.com[26]) in the interest of space and because the full version requires use of algorithms for accurate and quick scoring. To find your perfect match, you need to do two things:

1. Find your relationship personality. As we noted several times, there are four personality types: XX, XY, YX, and YY. The first letter represents your communication score, while the second represents your intimacy score. XX, for instance, indicates communication and intimacy scores that are both above 50 percent. An XY personality type would indicate scores above 50 percent in communication and below 50 percent in intimacy, as indicated by the Y on the right. Communication is always stated first in XY personality theory, but it is only half of the personality picture.

It may be sufficient for an individual to only know their personality type without delving into the levels of need, such as when taking the abbreviated version of the XY test presented in this book. But when it comes to matching, however, more is required. It requires an *expanded* version of the XY test and computer analysis to accurately handle the increased complexity.

2. Because XY theory is a needs-based model, it is important to determine not just individual personality type, but the level of communication or intimacy *needed*. If you know the level of your needs and what your needs are in relationships, you can more accurately match yourself with a partner who can meet those needs.

The free abbreviated test was initially intended to be taken on dates, on the run, at a restaurant, or at Starbucks, when time is a factor. If your partner does not "pass" this quick version of the XY Personality test and you're not a match such as (XX-XX), (XY-XY), (YY-YY), etc., there is no need to test further. However, if there is a match *or* if, in spite of a mismatch, you are determined to proceed with the relationship, then the expanded version with detailed results is an absolute must. If your date won't pass the first test, which is intended to test for a personality match, then he won't "pass" the (expanded) second test either, which provides information on your *level* of needs in that relationship. But finding out your exact differences will give you a starting point at which to begin to work on the relationship right away.

Why waste two, three, or even five years to find out your partner won't commit or your spouse won't change when a simple personality test can alert you to this probability from the start? Why waste even a year or six months to find out that your date who shows you a lot of affection or attention today won't be able to keep up the act tomorrow because this is not who he or she truly is? A simple XY Personality test could easily have told you this. Or maybe you don't want someone that's too emotional, or too talkative. XY Personality testing could have warned you about that, so the expanded version with detailed analysis is the needs assessment that will appeal to couples as well.

I am aware that many married couples who are already in XY relationships might feel that the die is already cast, but you are not without hope. In fact, if problems exist, XY theory strongly suggests that someone's needs are going unmet. The XY tests can tell if you are well matched to the person you are with, whether it be a girlfriend, boyfriend, or a husband. If you find that you are not, the XYTheory.com website will provide you with a forum to allow you to vent.[27] Most individuals in XY relationships have reported that XY venting helps. You will find others like you, venting about their experiences, sharing their concerns, and blogging about it. Another option is to participate in our 14-Week Program for XY couples. The program takes three to four months, depending on the severity of the relational problems. This program offers insight and techniques weekly that you and your partner can use to narrow the XY divide and make your relating to each other a more harmonious experience. This can be accessed through the XYTheory.com website as well.

If you're still single and use the Internet as a means of meeting Mr. Right, simply refuse to go on that first date without both of you taking the XY Personality test. You should at least know what you're up against. Most Internet dating sites do not allow you to check out your date or ask his friends about his personality quirks. XY testing can do that for you quite accurately. XY Personality tests match according to the most important factor in relationship success—personality…and not the social personality that often disappears once the honeymoon is over. Our XY Matchmaking site XYMatchQuest.com, does not focus on personal appearance, personal effects, or even personal interests—just relationship personality. This should be your first step.

Chapter 11

The Dangerous Test

Before the End

*I*ronically, a friend sent me a text the night before I began writing this chapter to tell me the steps she had taken to leave her marriage. She was a *high* X communicator and even *higher* on the scale of emotional needs. He was moderate on the communicator scale and low on the emotional scale. They had been married for some time, and their children were about to leave for college, so she was contemplating spending the next few decades of her life in the "empty nest"…without children, but alone with him. I suggested she hang in there for the children (I rarely do that). She sent this text in response:

'Hello dear John, well, well, well…

I'm done! I cannot be in a relationship with someone who tries to destroy the loving person that I am, and I also told him I don't plan to move out either. Deal with it!'

In chapter 2, I told you that the XY theory and test could predict whether your relationship would succeed or fail. It cannot tell you whether you will stay with your partner or leave. But it can tell you whether you're likely to, or if the probability that he would do so is high. My friend who sent me the text above filed for divorce one year later.

Here is where the XY theory departs from many other models. Other models claim that the final step of a relationship includes the departure of a partner or spouse. But having written this book in the midst of a deep recession, when many explained that they couldn't financially afford to leave, I can tell you that the end has more to do with one person in the relationship deciding that he or she is finished with it. Finished with trying, finished with pretending, or adjusting and finished with changing who they are for a partner. Putting an end to the acts of kindness, and the sacrifices for the sake of love.

The deeds X type partners provide are often seen by some Ys as acts of service, a duty, instead of acts of kindness. The problem with this is that Ys mistake a *service* for a *duty* and expects it will be continued contractually no matter how much he or she has hurt their partner. "After all, you don't quit going to work because your boss said something to hurt your feelings, do you?" one Y asked his wife. "Nor do you reduce the quota of work you're expected to do. Because it's your duty," he explained.

OK, let's take a look at these tests. Below is an abbreviated version of the XY Personality test. Remember that the accuracy of an abbreviated version will not be as high as the full version available on the XYTheory.com or XYMatchQuest. com websites. I encourage you to visit the sites and take that version of the test.

Also you are discouraged from any collaboration between you and your partner when taking the test. In fact, you should circle your answers separately and privately and get together for the scoring. Your two response choices are: "Somewhat agree or "somewhat disagree."

Test 1—Self (Partner 1)

The XY Personality test™
(Abbreviated)

Name: _____ Date: _____

For each of the following statements below, circle the answer that corresponds to your level of agreement or disagreement. Answer these questions as they relate to your current relationship. Note that you must be completely candid and honest for the results to be accurate.

If you're not in a current relationship, *after taking this test,* please go to test number 4 ("App Your Ex Test") to determine your ex partner's personality.

1. You do not believe it is important to respond to texts and phone messages immediately.

   a. Somewhat disagree   b. Somewhat agree

2. You do not believe it is helpful to the relationship for each of you to share your feelings often.

   a. Somewhat disagree   b. Somewhat agree

3. Your partner is taking a trip to visit family or friends. You do not believe it is necessary that your partner calls or texts you when he/she arrives, and stays in touch while he or she is away.

   a. Somewhat disagree   b. Somewhat agree

4. You do not believe it is necessary for partners to frequently say to each other, "I love you."

   a. Somewhat disagree   b. Somewhat agree

5. You have been accused of not being affectionate or passionate enough in your relationships.

   a. Somewhat disagree   b. Somewhat agree

6. You sometimes wish your partner would be quiet so you could have a few moments of silence.

   a. Somewhat disagree   b. Somewhat agree

7. Physical displays of affection such as hugging, handholding, and kissing are not that important to a relationship.

   a. Somewhat disagree   b. Somewhat agree

8. You believe conversation should serve a function or specific purpose, such as to share facts or information.

   a. Somewhat disagree   b. Somewhat agree

9. You do not believe receiving a call, text message, or e-mail from your partner is necessary during your work day, and wouldn't care for the interruption.

   a. Somewhat disagree   b. Somewhat agree

10. Sometimes when your partner is just chatting or asking a question, you're not sure whether he/she expects you to respond each time.

    a. Somewhat disagree   b. Somewhat agree

11. You are enjoying a solo activity (such as reading a novel, playing solitaire or a video game, etc.) and you are in deep concentration when your partner walks in and wants to talk. How do you react? You do not immediately stop what you are doing to engage in conversation with your partner.

    a. Somewhat disagree   b. Somewhat agree

12. At the end of the day, you are not likely to ask your partner how his or her day went.

    a. Somewhat disagree   b. Somewhat agree

13. Your partner(s) have accused you of being distant or emotionally disconnected in the relationship.

    a. Somewhat disagree   b. Somewhat agree

14. Generally, in your relationships, you believe your partner(s) are more nurturing to you than you are to them.

    a. Somewhat disagree   b. Somewhat agree

15. If your parent or close relative developed a terminal illness, you believe it would be OK if your partner wanted to be told only the basics.

    a. Somewhat disagree   b. Somewhat agree

16. It would not bother you if your partner didn't want to share his/her intimate feelings or emotions with you.

    a. Somewhat disagree   b. Somewhat agree

Please answer the following question and choose one response that best applies.

17. How many hours of television do you watch on average per week?

    a. 0 to 5 hrs   b. 6 to 15 hrs   c. 16 to 30 hrs

Scoring:

Follow the instructions below.

Communication. Score your "somewhat disagree" answers a five (5) and your "somewhat agree" answers a zero (0). Total your points to get your communication score. A score between 25 and 40 indicates an X type personality, while a score ranging from 0 to 15 indicates a Y type personality. If you score 20 points in communication, you're on the border-line and are neither fully in the X or Y camp. Until you do the more comprehensive test on our website, you should probably view yourself as borderline. The following questions should be totaled for your communication type score: Questions 1, 6, 8–12, and 15 for a maximum total of forty (40) points and a minimum of zero (0).

Intimacy. Score your "somewhat disagree" answers a five (5) and your "somewhat agree" answers a zero (0). Total your points to get your intimacy score. A score between 25 and 40 indicates an X type personality, while a score ranging from 0 to 15 indicates a Y type personality. If you score 20 points in intimacy, you're on the borderline and are neither fully in the X or Y camp. Until you do the more comprehensive test on our website, you should probably view yourself as borderline. The following questions correspond to your intimacy score: Questions 2–5, 7, 13–14, and 16 for a maximum total of forty (40) points and a minimum of zero (0).

On question 17, the number of hours of TV watching will give clues as to whether this may become an issue in a mixed XY relationship.

Test 2—Self (Partner 2)

The XY Personality test™
(Abbreviated)

Name: _____ Date: _____

For each of the following statements below, circle the answer that corresponds to your level of agreement or disagreement. Answer these questions as they relate to your current relationship. Note that you must be completely candid and honest for the results to be accurate.

1. You do not believe it is important to respond to texts and phone messages immediately.

    a. Somewhat disagree   b. Somewhat agree

2. You do not believe it is helpful to the relationship for each of you to share your feelings often.

    a. Somewhat disagree   b. Somewhat agree

3. Your partner is taking a trip to visit family or friends. You do not believe it is necessary that your partner calls or texts you when he/she arrives, and stays in touch while he or she is away.

    a. Somewhat disagree   b. Somewhat agree

4. You do not believe it is necessary for partners to frequently say to each other, "I love you."

   a. Somewhat disagree   b. Somewhat agree

5. You have been accused of not being affectionate or passionate enough in your relationships.

   a. Somewhat disagree   b. Somewhat agree

6. You sometimes wish your partner would be quiet so you could have a few moments of silence.

   a. Somewhat disagree   b. Somewhat agree

7. Physical displays of affection such as hugging, hand-holding, and kissing are not that important to a relationship.

   a. Somewhat disagree   b. Somewhat agree

8. You believe conversation should serve a function or specific purpose, such as to share facts or information.

   a. Somewhat disagree   b. Somewhat agree

9. You do not believe receiving a call, text message, or e-mail from your partner is necessary during your work day, and wouldn't care for the interruption.

   a. Somewhat disagree   b. Somewhat agree

10. Sometimes when your partner is just chatting or asking a question, you're not sure whether he/she expects you to respond each time.

    a. Somewhat disagree   b. Somewhat agree

11. You are enjoying a solo activity (such as reading a novel, playing solitaire or a video game, etc.) and you are in deep concentration when your partner walks in and wants to talk. How do you react? You do not immediately stop what you are doing to engage in conversation with your partner.

    a. Somewhat disagree   b. Somewhat agree

12. At the end of the day, you are not likely to ask your partner how his or her day went.

    a. Somewhat disagree   b. Somewhat agree

13. Your partner(s) have accused you of being distant or emotionally disconnected in the relationship.

    a. Somewhat disagree   b. Somewhat agree

14. Generally, in your relationships, you believe your partner(s) are more nurturing to you than you are to them.

    a. Somewhat disagree   b. Somewhat agree

15. If your parent or close relative developed a terminal illness, you believe it would be OK if your partner wanted to be told only the basics.

    a. Somewhat disagree   b. Somewhat agree

16. It would not bother you if your partner didn't want to share his/her intimate feelings or emotions with you.

    a. Somewhat disagree   b. Somewhat agree

Please answer the following question and choose one response that best applies.

17. How many hours of television do you watch on average per week?

    a. 0 to 5 hrs   b. 6 to 15 hrs   c. 16 to 30 hrs

Scoring:

Follow the instructions below.

Communication. Score your "somewhat disagree" answers a five (5) and your "somewhat agree" answers a zero (0). Total your points to get your communication score. A score between 25 and 40 indicates an X type personality, while a score ranging from 0 to 15 indicates a Y type personality. If you score 20 points in communication, you're on the border-line and are neither fully in the X or Y camp. Until you do the more comprehensive test on our website, you should probably view yourself as borderline. The following questions should be totaled for your communication type score: Questions 1, 6, 8–12, and 15 for a maximum total of forty (40) points and a minimum of zero (0).

Intimacy. Score your "somewhat disagree" answers a five (5) and your "somewhat agree" answers a zero (0). Total your points to get your intimacy score. A score between 25 and 40 indicates an X type personality, while a score ranging from 0 to 15 indicates a Y type personality. If you score 20 points in intimacy, you're on the borderline and are neither fully in the X or Y camp. Until you do the more comprehensive test on our website, you should probably view yourself as borderline. The following questions correspond to your intimacy score: Questions 2–5, 7, 13–14, and 16 for a maximum total of forty (40) points and a minimum of zero (0).

On question 17, the number of hours of TV watching will give clues as to whether this may become an issue in a mixed XY relationship.

Test 3—Reluctant Partner Test

XY Perception Test™
Reluctant Partner Version

Name: _____   Date: _____

For each of the following statements below, indicate the response that corresponds to your level of agreement or disagreement. Please answer these questions as they relate to your "reluctant" partner in your current relationship. This test is particularly useful when one's partner is refusing to take the test. When this occurs, you can complete this test for him or her. Note that you must be completely candid and honest for results to be accurate.

1. Your partner is taking a trip to visit family or friends. Your partner is likely to text you when he/she arrives and to stay in touch while he or she is away.

   a. Somewhat disagree   b. Somewhat agree

2. Your partner believes it is helpful to the relationship for each of you to share your feelings often.

   a. Somewhat disagree   b. Somewhat agree

3. Spontaneous, romantic gestures and little surprises are vital to a healthy relationship and communicate how partners feel about each other. Would your partner agree or disagree?

   a. Somewhat disagree   b. Somewhat agree

4. Your partner never secretively wishes that you would be quiet so he/she could have a few moments of silence.

   a. Somewhat disagree   b. Somewhat agree

5. Your partner believes it is important for partners to say to each other, "I love you" and does so, often enough.

   a. Somewhat disagree   b. Somewhat agree

6. Physical displays of affection such as hugging, hand-holding, and kissing are important to a relationship. Would your partner agree or disagree?

   a. Somewhat disagree   b. Somewhat agree

7. Your partner does not believe conversation should serve a function or specific purpose, such as to share facts or information.

   a. Somewhat disagree   b. Somewhat agree

8. Your partner believes that receiving a call, text message, or e-mail from you is desirable during the work day and would not mind the interruption.

   a. Somewhat disagree   b. Somewhat agree

9. When you are just chatting or asking a question, you are sure your partner will respond each time.

   a. Somewhat disagree   b. Somewhat agree

10. Your partner is doing an activity alone (such as reading a novel, playing solitaire or a video game, etc.) and is in deep concentration when you walk in and want to talk. Your partner immediately stops what he or she is doing and engages in conversation with you.

    a. Somewhat disagree   b. Somewhat agree

11. It is important to your partner that you ask how his or her day went.

    a. Somewhat disagree   b. Somewhat agree

12. Your partner believes a strong emotional connection is important to him or her.

    a. Somewhat disagree   b. Somewhat agree

13. Your partner believes he or she is more nurturing to you than you are to him or her.

    a. Somewhat disagree   b. Somewhat agree

14. If a close relative became seriously ill, your partner would prefer to know the details.

    a. Somewhat disagree   b. Somewhat agree

15. Your partner responds immediately or in a timely manner when you send a text, e-mail, or when you leave a voice-mail for him or her.

    a. Somewhat disagree   b. Somewhat agree

16. It would bother your partner if you didn't want to share your intimate feelings or emotions with him or her.

    a. Somewhat disagree   b. Somewhat agree

Please answer the following question and choose one response that best applies.

17. How many hours of television do you watch on average per week?

    a. 0 to 5 hrs   b. 6 to 15 hrs   c. 16 to 30 hrs

Is this a problem for either you or your partner? Yes   No

Scoring:

Follow the instructions below.

Communication. For this test, the scoring is in reverse. Score your "somewhat disagree" answers a zero (0) and your "somewhat agree" answers a five (5). Total your points separately to get your communication and intimacy score. A score between 25 and 40 indicates an X type personality, while a score ranging from 0 to 15 indicates a Y type personality. If you score 20 points in communication, you're on the borderline and are neither fully in the X or Y camp. Until you do the more comprehensive test on our website, you should probably view yourself as borderline. The following questions should be totaled for your communication type score: Questions 4, 7–11, 14, and 15 for a maximum total of forty (40) points and a minimum of zero (0).

Intimacy. For this test, the scoring is in reverse. Score your "somewhat disagree" answers a zero (0) and your "somewhat agree" answers a five (5). Total your points to get your intimacy score. A score between 25 and 40 indicates an X type personality, while a score ranging from 0 to 15 indicates a

Y type personality. If you score 20 points in intimacy, you're on the borderline and are neither fully in the X or Y camp. Until you do the more comprehensive test on our website, you should probably view yourself as borderline. The following questions correspond to your intimacy score: Questions 1–3, 5-6, 12–13, and 16 for a maximum total of forty (40) points and a minimum of zero (0).

On question 17, the number of hours of TV watching will give clues as to whether this may become an issue in a mixed XY relationship.

Test 4—"App Your Ex" Test

"App Your Ex" Test™

Name: _____ Date: _____

    For each of the following statements, indicate the response that corresponds to your level of agreement or disagreement. Please answer these questions as they relate to your partner in your ***previous*** relationship. This test is particularly useful when one's partner is no longer in the picture and you would like to know if an XY difference was the cause. Note that you must be completely candid, answering questions to the best of your recollection for results to be accurate.

1. Your partner took a trip to visit family or friends. He or she was likely to text you when he/she arrived and to stay in touch while away.

   a. Somewhat disagree   b. Somewhat agree

2. Your partner believed it was helpful to the relationship for each of you to share your feelings often.

   a. Somewhat disagree   b. Somewhat agree

3. Spontaneous, romantic gestures and little surprises are vital to a healthy relationship and communicate how partners feel about each other. Would your partner have agreed or disagreed?

   a. Somewhat disagree   b. Somewhat agree

4. Your partner never secretively wished that you would be quiet so he/she could have a few moments of silence.

   a. Somewhat disagree   b. Somewhat agree

5. Your partner believed it was important for partners to say to each other, "I love you" and did so, often enough.

   a. Somewhat disagree   b. Somewhat agree

6. Physical displays of affection such as hugging, hand-holding, and kissing are important to a relationship. Would your partner have agreed or disagreed with this?

   a. Somewhat disagree   b. Somewhat agree

7. Your partner did not believe that conversation should serve a function or specific purpose, such as to share facts or information only.

   a. Somewhat disagree   b. Somewhat agree

8. Your partner believed that receiving a call, text message, or e-mail from you was desirable during the work day and would have appreciated the interruption.

   a. Somewhat disagree   b. Somewhat agree

9. When you were just chatting or asking a question, your partner was likely to respond each time.

   a. Somewhat disagree   b. Somewhat agree

10. Your partner was doing an activity alone (such as reading a novel, playing solitaire or a video game, etc.) and was in deep concentration when you walked in and wanted to talk. Your partner would have immediately stopped what he or she was doing and engaged in conversation with you.

    a. Somewhat disagree   b. Somewhat agree

11. It was important to your partner that you asked how his or her day went.

    a. Somewhat disagree   b. Somewhat agree

12. Your partner believed that a strong emotional connection was important to him or her.

    a. Somewhat disagree   b. Somewhat agree

13. Your partner believed he or she was more nurturing to you than you were to him or her.

   a. Somewhat disagree   b. Somewhat agree

14. If a close relative became seriously ill, your partner would have preferred to know the details.

   a. Somewhat disagree   b. Somewhat agree

15. Your partner would get back to you immediately or in a timely manner when you sent a text, e-mail, or when you left a voicemail for him or her.

   a. Somewhat disagree   b. Somewhat agree

16. It would have bothered your partner if you didn't want to share your intimate feelings or emotions with him or her.

   a. Somewhat disagree   b. Somewhat agree

Please answer the following question and choose one response that best applies.

17. How many hours of television do you watch on average per week?

   a. 0 to 5 hrs   b. 6 to 15 hrs   c. 16 to 30 hrs

Was this a problem for either you or your partner? Yes   No

Scoring:

Follow the instructions below.

Communication. For this test, the scoring is in reverse. Score your "somewhat disagree" answers a zero (0) and your "somewhat agree" answers a five (5). Total the points to get your Ex partner's communication score. A score between 25 and 40 indicates an X type personality, while a score ranging from 0 to 15 indicates a Y type personality. If your Ex scores 20 points in communication, he/she was on the borderline and was neither fully in the X or Y camp. Until you do the more comprehensive test on our website, you should probably view your Ex as borderline. The following questions should be totaled for the communication type score: Questions 4, 7–11, 14, and 15 for a maximum total of forty (40) points and a minimum of zero (0).

Intimacy. For this test, the scoring is in reverse. Score your "somewhat disagree" answers a zero (0) and your "somewhat agree" answers a five (5). Total the points to get your Ex partner's intimacy score. A score between 25 and 40 indicates an X type personality, while a score ranging from 0 to 15 indicates a Y type personality. If your Ex scores 20 points in intimacy, he/she was on the borderline and was neither fully in the X or Y camp. Until you do the more comprehensive test on our website, you should probably view your Ex as borderline. The following questions correspond to your Ex's intimacy score: Questions 1–3, 5-6, 12–13, and 16 for a maximum total of forty (40) points and a minimum of zero (0).

On question 17, the number of hours of TV watching will give clues as to whether this may have been an issue in a mixed XY relationship.

Now that you have taken the test, you may want to find a computer with an Internet connection and take the full version. The complex algorithms needed to calculate your personality type and level of need are beyond the scope of what is possible in this book, but a code is provided (7777) that will allow you to go to XYTheory.com or to the dating website, XYMatchQuest.com to complete and receive the results of your test. If your partner is unwilling to take the test, the websites also contain an unabbreviated XY Reluctant Partner Test. But as mentioned earlier, this abbreviated version of the XY test was provided for your use if (i) your partner refuses to complete the test, or (ii) you're between relationships, and you suspect an XY personality difference was the cause of your breakup. You can complete the test for your Ex and compare scores with your test. The Reluctant Partner version (test 3) presented here is only an abbreviated version to be used to increase awareness and is not as accurate a measure. However, a more accurate version is available on XYTheory. com or XYMatchQuest.com. The full version of the Reluctant Partner Test allows for a 95 percent accuracy rate because after spending some time with a partner, you learn to interpret their needs quite successfully, and you unconsciously tap into this knowledge when completing the test. If you don't have immediate access to a computer, don't despair. You can use your cell phone as well. Here again is the breakdown of the communication and intimacy table: this is a needs-based model. Your X and Y personality is reported as levels of need, *not numbers*, making it extremely difficult for self-scoring. But you can easily get a good idea of where you are relative to your partner.

Here are the possible levels of need:

100	_____	Extremely High Need
X	_____	High Need
X	_____	Moderate Need
50	_____	Borderline Need
Y	_____	Low Need
Y	_____	Extremely Low Need

We've put this chapter after 10 other chapters, explaining exactly what X and Y type personalities look like, so that even without completing this test, you could have a sense as to whether you have a high need to communicate (High X) or a low need (Low Y); a high need for intimacy (High Emotional X) or a low need for intimacy (Un-Emotional Y). But for more accuracy, we encourage you to take 10 minutes to log on at XYTheory.com or XYMatchQuest.com, put in the code when you register, and take your free self or matching test. (The code is 7777.)

What's in the Basket or Box

Critical to all romance is the need to know what's really in your partner's secret basket. You will recall from chapters 5 and 6 that both X and Y types have secondary needs which, when met, increase feelings of closeness or intimacy. As we said earlier, some men who discovered they were X types felt the label might feminize them, rob them of their alpha male membership cards, or in some way encourage their Y type females to say to them, "Why don't you *man up*?" So I promised them I'd put their traits in a toolbox instead of a basket. So here goes:

Because few people are 100% X or Y, which means we can still have a few traits from either side, it will be helpful for both of you to fill out each of these lists. For X type men and women, we said the following needs are in their basket or box:

	<u>Hers</u> (Partner 1) (Check off what you think your partner needs here)	<u>His</u> (Partner 2) (Check off what you think your partner needs here)
1. Affection	_____	_____
2. Attention	_____	_____
3. Affirmation/ Reassurance	_____	_____

4. Connectedness   _____   _____

5. Accountability   _____   _____

6. Verbal Expression of
   Emotion (VEE)   _____   _____

7. Romance   _____   _____

8. Public Display of
   Affection   _____   _____

9. Help (Mostly Domestic)   _____   _____

10. Gifts and Surprises   _____   _____

11. Proximity   _____   _____

12. Empathy / Sensitivity   _____   _____

13. Personal Display of
    Emotion (to Partner,
    mostly)   _____   _____

14. Value   _____   _____

Example:

             √√
_____   _____

Now, each of you should have placed a check mark next to the need you believe your partner would like to receive from you. Do this exercise for both X needs (1–14) and Y needs (1–10) for each of you. You can put two check marks to denote greater need.

There are several discoveries we'll make here. (1) You can determine: Who knew their partner best and why? (Don't be embarrassed about this result. I myself had only two correct when I did this with someone I'd dated for 2 years.) (2) Discuss what made you assume your partner needed something he or she didn't need. (3) Sensitively talk about the (√√) double marks, the greater needs. (We will work on these some more using our Workshop for XY Couples via the Internet).[28] Don't be afraid to write on the pages. It is important and eye-opening to actually see this in writing. This exercise does not include a total score; each item is important to the individual and will be discussed. There are couples who have been together for years without knowing that boyfriends or husbands who love them dearly *hated* their public display of affection, or their need to be reassured of their love—simply because it was not ever discussed. So, discuss it. Please. This is your opportunity. You cannot guess at these specific issues like you can about a partner's overall need for intimacy or communication. You've got to ask.

And now to the Y's:

	Hers (Partner 1)	His (Partner 2)
	(Check off what you think your partner needs here)	(Check off what you think your partner needs here)
1. Common Interests	_____	_____
2. Solitude / Quiet	_____	_____

3. Time Alone
_____   _____

4. Space
_____   _____

5. Actions
_____   _____

6. Compatibility
_____   _____

7. Shared Activity
_____   _____

8. Novelty
_____   _____

9. Privacy
_____   _____

10. Loyalty / Trust
_____   _____

Remember, novelty refers to the need of many Ys to have newness in their lives, excitement in their relationship and marriages—excitement that literally produces chemicals in the bloodstream that strengthen their bonds. But Xs can have this need too, so you should both complete the list on each other.

If any of the other secondary needs are foggy or unclear to you because we discussed many other concepts since the secondary needs (in chapters 5 and 6), please go back. Re-read chapters 5 and 6 and review the full meaning of the ones you forgot. If as an X type, you're reading this book alone and had to choose one section to help your Y type partner know who he or she is, and you desperately would like to give them an out emotionally, then this section is it. Here, we discuss traits that will eventually either draw you closer to your partner or push your partner away from you. If you are overwhelming him or her with your nonfunctional, trivial, chit-chatty conversation, over-the-top emotional outbursts and drama or high emotional needs, these secret items in the basket and box, if discussed sensitively, have the potential to give your relationship and *you* the *rescue* you deserve.

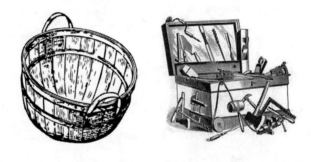

Basket   Toolbox

Needs Assessment Exercise

Finally, each of you should write 3 unknown needs or desires not mentioned on our list of traits that you have placed checkmarks next to. List these under the picture of the basket above, and your partner can list his needs under the toolbox. There are needs that make a difference to marital and relationship satisfaction that your partner doesn't know about because you've never mentioned them to him or her.

One X type woman told her husband she wanted him to stalk her if he needed to, but to do something, anything, to show that she mattered to him. Did she really *want* to encourage stalking? Probably not. But at least now he knew he needed to do much more to *show* his wife that he cared.

Chapter 12

The Chemical Affair

*Y*our best friend set you up on a date with a man your age. You're a little skeptical because she tried to set you up before a few weeks ago and that ended badly. However, this date was quite good-looking, about 6 feet tall, well-built, had a good job, making a salary in the high six-figures. You were attracted to him the moment he walked in the room, and learning that he was a neurosurgeon didn't hurt at all. He had a brain, after all, but as the evening wore on, you slowly but surely lost interest in this attractive prospect. Why? He ogled every female who passed by and tried to do it subtly, thinking you wouldn't notice. What you did notice is that he didn't appear that into you. So you asked yourself why? You're not at all bad looking, so you wondered what went wrong this time. Before long you begin to count the minutes for this date to end.

Fast forward two weeks. Long enough for you to agree to go out on yet another dating "expedition" as your friend calls it, but not long enough for you to forget the last guy—the "I think I'm God's gift to women" neurosurgeon. The irony is, this guy your friend wants you to go out with is your last date's cousin! What are the chances, you ask, for cousins to *not be* the same type of jerks you are no longer interested in dating? You ponder this until he walks into the restaurant and you are again stopped by his stature and good looks but stumped by how much he looks like the surgeon-cousin you met two weeks before. You're convinced your best friend played an ugly trick on you and sent you his twin—until he opens his mouth to introduce himself to you and you *don't* detect a hint of the cockiness and arrogance of which his first cousin reeked.

This fellow is polite and engaging, more interested in asking about you than in talking about himself. Like a southern gentleman, he actually stands up to get your chair and doesn't sit down at the table until you do. More importantly, though you've just met, he seems oblivious to the other gorgeous women in the room but is *quite focused on you.*

As the date goes on, you become more convinced of the other things your best friend said about him. Small details such as the fact that, though he was built like a Greek god, when it comes to choosing a mate he could not be less concerned with a woman's looks.

He is more concerned about personality than appearance. He pampers and spoils the woman he's with. Once he commits to someone, he is totally monogamous. He doesn't have roaming eyes. In fact, he avoids even the appearance of unfaithfulness or cheating by avoiding the company of other females. Before the date is over, he explains that he has some cousins living on the eastside that he doesn't want to be confused with. They "play the field," run around with several women, and specialize in one-night-stands, with no thought about who they hurt. More than a few of them have fathered children out of wedlock and never stick around to parent their offspring, let alone pay child support to the struggling mothers. You nod knowingly, as you remember your best friend sharing about his previous relationship with a woman with two very small children he cared for as if they were his own—while the paternal father of those children could not care enough to put in an appearance and was in and out of prison.

From all appearances, you two seem to have the makings of a perfect match. A classic XX couple perhaps, with all that it takes to sustain a relationship that can stand the test of time and possibly last forever. Remember, only 3 percent of mammal species, including humans, form monogamous relationships. So these two are likely to be in the lucky 3 percent.

Unfortunately, the couple and the cousins you just read about were *not* among them. There's a huge problem with this story. These handsome cousins were not real men.

You were reading about a species of *rodents* called voles. The prairie voles, for example, practice monogamy in a way that would put many human counterparts to shame. Their mountain-dwelling cousins, the Montane Voles, are promiscuous playboys, and within the last decade, scores of studies have been done on these rodents in the hope of finding clues to human sexuality and, more importantly, monogamy.

Is Your Lover a Rat?

As it turns out, the cousin—the Montane Vole, which is not monogamous—has more in common with a house mouse or a garden variety rat than with the prairie vole. The males do not bond after sex; they do not stick around to pamper their mates, as their monogamous cousins do; and they will not stick around to help raise the pups they fathered before taking off to their next conquest.

By contrast, prairie voles form long-lasting relationships with each other. One male chooses one female. Or, more accurately, one female chooses one male with little or no concern for appearance. In their society, the runt would have a pretty good chance of having a family (as scientists have found that little or no attention is paid to the body mass of the male during pair bonding). The pair sets it off with a 24-hour sex marathon in the "nest," after which they are bonded for life (no worries about whether the guy in this relationship is a "love-em and leave-em" type).

After this, they prefer to spend all their time together, grooming and pampering each other for hours on end. They avoid meeting other potential mates from here on, and the male becomes an aggressive protector of his partner. Males and females nest together and have babies, and the male vole spends as much time taking care of those babies as the female does, both as attentive and care-providing as the other.

Unlike the prairie vole, his cousin the Montane vole skips out on his mate as soon as she is pregnant, and never looks back.

With so many scientific experiments that have benefited humans beginning with mice in a researcher's lab, it was just a matter of time before researchers would investigate the neurobiology of these two rodent species to see why they demonstrate such different social and romantic behavior, and whether their findings could be applied to human behavior. As it turns out, a small handful of genes and hormones are responsible for the commitment-prone voles, while the absence of the same are responsible for the promiscuity of the womanizing Montanes.

Study after study has shown that the hormones *oxytocin* in the female and *vasopressin* in the male—released during and before sex—activates receptors in the brain that are involved with pleasure and reward. These are the same areas in the brain that are activated by cocaine and amphetamines and are responsible, along with oxytocin facilitated releases of dopamine, for the addictive features of sex.

There is a caveat to all this, however. The oxytocin and vasopressin are also responsible for *bonding* in prairie voles. If these hormones are blocked before their absorption by receptors in the brain, the very same monogamous, commitment-loving, one-woman vole becomes like his playboy cousin and will not settle down or become the family man his genes meant him to be. Interestingly, researchers discovered that if voles are injected with the hormone oxytocin, kept in a cage *near* the female, but prevented from having sex—they still showed a preference for family and companionship with that one female. (So much for the case many guys keep making about needing to have sex to "kick" off the relationship and seal the deal!)

Up the Food Chain

Scientists took experimentation a step further, to see whether injecting the Montane voles with oxytocin and vasopressin could make them more like their well-behaved, romantic cousins. Sorry ladies (X type ladies that is). It did not make a difference, and gave a clue to the complexity of treating higher-order animals—including humans—with doses of oxytocin to improve social behavior. The Montane vole's behavior did not improve because their cousins, the prairie voles, had receptors for oxytocin and vasopressin in reward centers of the brain to absorb the oxytocin, while the Montanes did not.

Larry Young is a researcher in social attachment at Emory University in Atlanta, Georgia, at the Center for Behavioral Neuroscience. Young believes that prairie voles stay together because they get "a natural high" from being with their mates, while the Montane voles do not.[29] What causes the difference, then, is not only how much oxytocin and vasopressin are released—the hormones that play a large role in social bonding and romantic attachments—but in the location (and, some scientists believe, the density) of the receptor cells that respond to these "love" hormones.

Other experiments have been done on primates. Monogamous marmosets, for instance, were found to have higher levels of vasopressin than the *non-monogamous* rhesus macaques. What we have seen so far seems to lend evidence to the hypothesis we began to put forward in chapter 1: If indeed hormones play a part in mammalian social attachments, then perhaps when it comes to bonding, commitment, empathy, attachments, fidelity, and monogamy, the common factor appears to be not the sex of the mammal but the brain structure with regard to hormones and the receptors for those hormones.

One woman with whom I shared some of this data concluded that her husband must share brain structure with the prairie voles (though not brain size!). She boasted of his faithfulness for the 20 years they had been married, his attentiveness to her, and his disinterest in even so much as looking at other sexier or more beautiful women. But when she later learned that he indeed had a mistress and maintained the secret affair for 10 of those 20 years of marriage, she accosted me and shouted that these studies on oxytocin were incorrect. I reminded her that she had left before I could get to the part about noted exceptions and variability in infidelity among *some* prairie voles that strayed.

Dr. Steven Phelps, an associate of Dr. Young at Emory University, found quite a lot of variation in the distribution of vasopressin receptors in the brains of individual prairie voles and suggests that this likely accounts for unexpected differences in their social behavior and attachments.[30] Moreover, humans tend to be the most complex of mammals when it comes to predictable romantic behavior, with a host of variables that don't even begin to play a role in the behavior of lower animals. In other words, factors beyond mere hormones, such as human choice, often determine whether we stay or play. Every interaction we engage in as human beings is more complex, where the actual behavior is not to be the only focus, but why the individual behaved the way he or she did and how that individual feels about it when confronted after. This is where there is a lot more consistency between Xs and Ys, with a lot more emotion and angst on the part of the X and a lot less genuinely expressed regret or remorse on the part of many Ys.

At Florida State University, researchers have found that exposure to the opposite sex in prairie voles, causes new nerve cells to be generated in the brain. They hypothesize that this memory, which is mostly olfactory (where rodents identify their mate's odor), is the rodent equivalent of remembering a personality and may become an imprint linked with pleasure. Helen Fisher, a researcher at Rutgers University, contends that love comes in three stages, or levels, which we can participate in singularly or collectively.[31] These are lust (i.e., Montane voles), romantic love, and social attachment (i.e., prairie voles). Dopamine is most implicated in the first stage, the infatuation stage, where lust plays a role. She hypothesizes that this explains why couples who participate in new activities together have the added benefit of a dopamine (addictive) rush, which facilitates the longevity of the relationship. This matches the needs of Y types who require new and non-monotonous activities to continually foster bonding, and seems to support XY theory.

At this point, we are unable to decipher by a blood test whether our boyfriends, husbands, or wives have hormone levels that support long-term bonding—in other words, it is impossible to determine a person's true intentions or inclinations. Not only are we as humans so complex that we often are unclear about our own intentions, but we must contend with hormones and other unconscious motivations. It should be noted that Dr. Zak, a neuroscientist living in Loma Linda, California, has done considerable research on oxytocin levels in human beings and has been able to manipulate men and women to demonstrate more empathy (a side-effect of oxytocin) as well as generosity and trust.[32]

He had to go to great lengths to get approval for a version of the drug that he could legally use in clinical trials, but his work involved mostly a "trust" game he devised. One exception to this was an experiment he did at a wedding where he took blood samples of the bride, groom, and many of their guests. He found that oxytocin levels in the blood were the highest in those most closely associated with or related to the newlyweds, tapering off the farther removed individuals were from the marrying pair. Not surprisingly, the bride had considerably more oxytocin in her blood than her groom had, because testosterone (occurring naturally in men in larger quantities) has been known to deplete oxytocin levels.

What was interesting is Dr. Zak's research conclusion about levels of testosterone not occurring predictably in males versus females, as some women had more testosterone than their men. His conclusion? It's not good science to stereotype personalities along gender lines because hormones, like testosterone, could not be predicted, and we now know that testosterone affects oxytocin (which he has dubbed the moral molecule). This appears to confirm our hypothesis in chapter 1: that personalities need a new designation that abandons traditional gender lines (we went with X and Y), and changes in society that we first thought were only sociological and psychological now appear to also be chemical and biological.

Notwithstanding, dopamine and other hormones make the sexual experience quite an addicting experience—but this does not solve our problems; rather, it compounds them. Most animals are addicted to sex hormones such as dopamine. Oxytocin, vasopressin, and a cocktail of other drugs act on the same area of the brain responsible for drug addictions and generate the same euphoria that a cocaine high does. Research done by scientists at the University of London found that the brains of people who claim to have fallen deeply in love do not look like brains that experience strong emotions but rather look like "brains on crack."[15]

Falling in love and the euphoria it produces use the same neural pathways that are activated during addiction. This fact comes with a warning: How careful we must be with whom we choose to fall in love, and when. And this warning goes out particularly to X type personalities in general and emotional Xs in particular. If oxytocin is playing a role in the *chemistry* of X types, who find it easier to bond than their Y type partners do—it is no wonder that X types often prefer to change who they are and adapt to the person they're with than walk away.

Beverly, one of my clients, called just yesterday to tell me between sobs how she had lost all dignity and self-respect to be with her Y type lover, who had done everything to "hurt her and get rid of her, except to kick her in her teeth."

"Why can't I leave him, John?" she pleaded. "He's no good for me. He tells me he doesn't love me all the time, but I feel deep down inside he just doesn't know it yet." Then she flip-flops. "No, he must not love me if he openly cheats on me with other girls." She continued, "John, please don't judge me. Don't think less of me because I'm a pathetic excuse for a human being. My parents would be so ashamed of me. I go to work while my man stays at home and plays video games, talks to other girls on Facebook, looks at Internet porn, and says he's spending his time on the golf course, even though I don't believe he could name the different clubs. What's wrong with me? How did I get this way?" I reminded her about the addictive power of the hormones she was dealing with and the fact that baby steps are what were needed to get away.

One study showed that for those with high oxytocin levels, most of which goes into production during sex, even hearing their lover's voice; smelling his cologne as they walk through the mall; going to their familiar special places; or naturally meeting with him, seeing the individual, or being physically close, is enough to trigger secretions of oxytocin. All of these would need to be avoided for at least 72 hours before the bonding attachment of oxytocin or vasopressin would even begin to subside. This explains why (as it is for other addictions), the first few days and weeks of a breakup are the most painful and difficult emotionally.

Research also indicates that we are guided by love maps. Whether loving someone deeply shapes our brains, as it does with prairie voles, or not, scientists are convinced that some imprinting occurs in that our first sexual experiences leave an imprint, a sort of map that communicates to us what kind of relationship we should expect, including what we should expect in a partner. For XY theory, this is not a comforting discovery. This would mean that people in general tend to repeat their mistakes romantically because they're more powerfully drawn to what is familiar than to what is compatible. X and Y types will do the same. It may take you (like it did me) several bites of the apple before you're convinced that when it comes to relational personality, you're better off going with your personality type than rolling the dice.

Chemistry and the Chemical Affair

I have yet to talk about the role chemistry, chemicals, and genetics play in bonding without having at least one person in the group ask if I know of a pill they can buy, or a spray they can use on their husband or wife to make him or her more to their liking. At the time of this writing, such pills and sprays were in clinical trials only and not intended to be commercially available to unhappy lovers. That may change one day.

Others have asked me about a blood test to check vasopressin levels. Keep in mind that research work has not yet been sufficiently conducted on humans to make a determination of that kind (though it has in rodents). But some promising studies *have* been done. One small study in particular delivered oxytocin via a spray in the nostrils of two dozen men who were given pre- and post-tests on empathy. Empathy is the type of emotion that would cause your partner to treat you the way he would want to be treated by you. The researchers and the partners of those men reported a post-test increase in empathy (kinder and more sensitive) to their mates with an increase in communication as an unexpected side effect. Furthermore, Dr. Zak's research reports an increase in generosity, which translates to a more reciprocal relationship, where there is give and take between partners, of all the elements needed to build intimacy and trust. Increases in trust, reciprocation, intimacy and communication are the factors that make up the basis of XY theory, and here is a drug that can increase all! And what about the woman who bought a two-story home for the sole purpose of having at least a floor to separate her from her extra talkative X man? Should she slip something in his drink to *decrease* his bonding hormones? Some testosterone, perhaps?

Maybe hormone therapy for human use is just around the corner. Scientists and pharmaceutical companies are already talking about a form of oxytocin that can be used to treat autism. Remember social communication (pragmatic language) and intimacy are low areas for children with autism. Oxytocin could easily become their miracle drug if early trials prove successful and can be replicated around the world.

As far as getting what we want, scientists at Binghamton University in New York conducted a study on 181 young adults and found that differences in their DNA were linked to their sexual behavior, particularly in the area of fidelity or faithfulness. A certain variant of the DRD4 gene was implicated as the cause for their decisions to have more one-night stands than those without the gene, as well as longer adulterous affairs. This gene controls how much dopamine is released during sex, making sex more addicting for some than others. At the time of this writing, this study has yet to be replicated, though Dr. Bonnie Weil, PhD, will cite it and feel somewhat vindicated because it fits predictions she made.[33] She has said for years that men who cheat may have higher levels of vasopressin, which might cause higher frequency of high-risk behaviors. The DRD4 gene is also believed to be related to other thrill-seeking behaviors, such as gambling, drinking, and extreme sports. The good doctor goes on to quickly point out that a genetic disposition is not a compulsion but a choice. Disposition is not destiny.

So what do men and women really want? And will knowing about the role of chemicals, affect the way we feel about our partners? This chapter raises more questions than answers.

- If you believed the research presented in this chapter, can you be completely unforgiving of an adulterer with a strong genetic disposition to cheat?
- If higher levels of dopamine are implicated in acts of infidelity and you could, through a blood test, prove that your partner's levels are astronomically high, would this soften your position concerning any of the acts of sexual indiscretions committed by your partner?
- Husbands, if you could prove that those headaches your wife claimed to have as the reason for her not delivering

on her "wifely duties" were indeed caused by low libido, in turn caused by low hormone production—would you consider softening on your demands for her participation in an activity she could only minimally enjoy?

- If you had to vote one day for the government to allow sale of a drug that would make boyfriends commit to their girlfriends, make husbands better fathers, and reduce acts of infidelity, would you do it?

- Do you feel that if a *blood test* were available—that could predict not the certainty but the likelihood that your partner would cheat, or drag you along in a relationship for years and not be able to commit—you would want it to be mandatory in your state or province? How about just available to couples who wanted it?

- If it is discovered one day that XX type men and women have more naturally produced oxytocin and vasopressin than their more socially detached and aloof YY type partners, would you agree to a blood test to determine your lover's relational personality type? How about just a quick personality test to replace the more intrusive blood test? Maybe the *XY Personality test*?

Closing Considerations

1. When it comes to predicting chemical affairs, the context should certainly be considered. Researchers believe oxytocin improves cooperativeness, social affiliation, and trust by improving the social awareness of those administered the drug. But the context makes this tricky. Would you still want your partner to be more aware and attentive socially if he or she comes to the table with trust issues. What if he or she suffers from a personality disorder like borderline personality disorder that comes ready-made with characteristics such as boundary issues, mistrust, and at times, mood swings and logic impairment? Though the goal is to build trust and to bond, the very goal is thwarted by the means that oxytocin utilizes to achieve its goals. In other words, for some, oxytocin would be an example of "ends that don't justify the means."

2. We've alluded to it several times with the Montane voles, but simply administering vasopressin to a man who cheats or has commitment and sensitivity issues will not, in and of itself, be guaranteed to fix these ills. In addition to considering the complexity of human interaction, the effects of one's past experiences or early childhood, and so forth; keep in mind that Montane voles (the playboys) were unchanged by vaso-

pressin administrations because of a lack of adequate receptors in the brain. The same may be true of human subjects.

3. Finally, there is individual personality. Some hormone treatments can potentially make recipients more aggressive. Also, some studies showed a sexual satiety among subjects. That would mean that if your partner already suffers from low libido, the side effect of hormone treatment might be the opposite of what you hoped for by further reducing it. Also, other studies with hormone therapy produced subjects who became lethargic, unmotivated, and uncompetitive. Diminished social behavior was also noted when individuals dealt with unfamiliar situations or people. But often, attention to detail was increased.

So if what you want is for your man to notice the change in your makeup and hairstyle, well, with a little spray of vasopressin, you've got it. But hormones can't make him like what he's noticing for the first time, or force him to be *gentle* in telling you how he really feels about you if he is no gentleman at all.

Chapter 13

Putting the "Y" in Intimacy

W e learned in chapter 3 that "X" types bond by talking and touching. Girlfriends, and wives with partners who *talk* enough will likely still be dissatisfied with their mates, if they did not *touch* enough. But let's get straight to the physical intimacy, shall we? For X types, intimacy (touch) is a form of communication and bonding, which means that X type women are less likely to engage in sex for recreational purposes. The reason why author Steve Harvey, in his book, advised women to "date like a man" is simply that he presupposes that men, and men alone, know how to detach emotionally during intimacy.[34] The premise of XY theory says, instead, don't spend years in therapy learning how to change who you are to suit the stereotype of what men are believed to be. Don't force yourself to be aloof and detached in relationships like the men many self-help gurus believe "men" tend to be. Don't change *who* you are to get *who* you want. Go out there and find someone just like you. Find an X type male who is like you. Find a man who is likely to share your values and put the same value on your body as you do.

Find a woman who likes to be romanced or not. A woman who likes to chit-chat like you do, or likes her quiet and solitude like you do. But please find someone whose ultimate goal is not to use you instrumentally so he or she can have you as a convenience. Find someone like you!—because people just like you are everywhere.

Twenty to thirty years ago, research showed that men were more likely to cheat, more likely to have extramarital affairs, more likely to engage in emotional infidelity, than their female companions. Naturally, the entrance of women in the workforce during the feminist and liberation movements of the 1970s and 1980s is partly responsible for changing that. As we covered in chapter 1, the shift among young people from the traditional roles expected of boys to nontraditional roles, which led to a choice of career paths that are decidedly more gender neutral today than they were thirty years ago, is also a major contributor. Today research is showing that infidelity among women is on the rise—and, according to some studies, is right on par with infidelity among men.

Montane voles are unlike their nurturing, homebuilding cousins in the prairie who practice monogamy. Some women who were tested at the Institute and had at least one Y factor, either in communication or intimacy, often showed less concern for fidelity, and even less when the Y factor fell in the domain of emotions or intimacy. One Y type woman explained that when it comes to dating and sex, she is very much aware that she dates like a man, but she can't help herself. She doesn't feel that close bond to a guy after she's had sex with him, and she does not have to force herself to "think" like a man or to behave like him.

The fact that Y types can have sex for purely physical and recreational reasons is just half the story. Remember dopamine? One of the hormones produced in large quantities in the rodents who were tested? It was absorbed by the same receptors in the brain that would absorb and be affected by cocaine and other narcotics, and was the hormone that made voles and other mammals addicted to sex in the way cocaine makes addicts of human beings. OK, you remember. Well, dopamine levels rise about 50 percent during sex, and dopamine is responsible for you and your partner wanting "it" all the time as well. It is these drugs that bring many men (and women) back to each other repeatedly. But dopamine has very little of the bonding properties that oxytocin does, so if he can't get his fix from you and he doesn't feel bonded to you... well, you get the picture.

Why Y's Can Hit It and Quit It

But to what is your partner really addicted? We've found that Ys are often more addicted to sex, while X types are more addicted to the individual they've had sex with. What's true for prairie voles is also true for higher mammals such as monkeys and men. Oxytocin production, whose main feature is bonding, could be more instrumental in X to X type bonding during sex because both sexes also enjoy a dopamine rush. The only difference is that for some individuals, the addiction appears to be not just to the activity but to the individual with whom they engage in the activity. Simply walking away after sex appears to be much less of an option for them.

The men whom Steve Harvey wants you to pattern your dating habits after appear more and more to be Y type men! Studies to confirm this are underway, with new oxytocin research on humans surfacing every month.

We, at The Jacob Research Institute, will keep you posted on our website.[35] Suffice it to say, perhaps, that the more pertinent question to ask is not "if I sleep with him, will he still leave me?," but rather "if I do, does he have a personality type that makes it less likely for him to stay?"

Sex as a Shared Activity

I am not a fisherman. In fact, I must have gone fishing no more than twice in my entire life. The only time my college friends could convince me to come along, they had to promise me, the non-fisherman, that I was guaranteed to catch something. I did. I caught one small fish, in a pond teaming with many larger ones. It wasn't until I got home with my small catch that my college mates informed me that the pond was a fishing reserve, stocked with trout—left a little hungry to ensure that those who paid to fish there would be sure to make a catch. I must tell you, I never went back. That one experience was good enough for me. There was no thrill in an easy catch. And though I can't say that I enjoy tasks that present near insurmountable odds, the opposite is as distasteful and unexciting. I may be somewhere in the middle when it comes to fishing, but Y types are generally not. Y types enjoy a challenge and are apt to walk away from an easy catch.

It would seem that the best way for you, an X type, to tell whether the person sitting across the table from you is a monogamous prairie vole or a promiscuous cousin is to make that individual wait before becoming intimate or physical. But it's not that simple. Many self-help authors have suggested keeping new partners waiting for sex as a test. This is not new. If for Ys, sex is an activity used for recreation rather than bonding, then the advice to wait is useful. But even here, hormones play a role. Testosterone is implicated in heightened sex drive and is, according to some studies, 10 times higher in men than in women (in other studies, it's as much as 18 times higher). This explains in part why complaints about too little sex generally come from the males in the relationship.

For the Y type male with more testosterone and less oxytocin, *precommitment* sex actually destroys your chances of ever getting a commitment because commitment is tied in with high oxytocin levels. On the other hand, medal-winning Olympic athletes tend to have higher levels of testosterone than their losing counterparts. The thrill of the win increases testosterone levels. Y type males who view sex as a conquest will—like the winner of an Olympic track meet, or the one who prevails to win the job promotion—experience a spike in testosterone, which inhibits the absorption of oxytocin. This will mean lower oxytocin in the blood and will drastically lower your chances of bonding with him or having him feel attached to you in any way *after* you've given your all to him.

Remember, everything comes down to what his view of sex is, and how he views you. Are you a once-in-a-lifetime catch, someone to be cherished and respected, or a notch on his belt? Is he in that age 30+ period of his life where he has sown his wild oats, had enough sex as sport, and is more likely to want to settle down, than to treat sexual encounters as testosterone-spiking personal conquests?

Cohabitation

This is a good time to talk about cohabitation, or the rise of unmarried partners living together. Statistics show cohabitation is on an incredible rise worldwide (but more so in Western nations). It's also true that a large percentage of cohabitants "slide" into cohabitation. First, you spend a night at your girlfriend's or boyfriend's apartment. It's not planned. You didn't bring a toothbrush and certainly weren't brazen enough to walk with a change of clothes. No need to worry. Your new partner has an extra toothbrush. One night becomes a weekend, and a weekend becomes a week. Before you know it, you have your own drawer in the chest of drawers and a corner in the closet. You have become a "slider," according to the experts. Someone who just sorta fell into cohabitation unintentionally.

Others are more formal in walking into this arrangement with eyes wide open. It's like a marriage proposal, brought up over a nice dinner or in the throes of romance and agreed on by all parties. Here is where we must talk about XY theory.

Cohabitation is not commitment! X type personalities have been lulled into putting up a little longer with reluctant partners, under the assumption that only a serious partner would take such a big step to live together. After all the cajoling from you to get married, the Y type throws you a bone and says, "OK, let's get an apartment together. I can see us happy in our own flat." Nothing could be farther from the truth. It would help for X types to ask their Y type partner what their reasons are for wanting to live together and (if interested in marriage) what their timeline is for marriage. Many won't ask this at the point of moving in, for fear of being interpreted as overly anxious or seemingly desperate.

However, many studies now show that living together does not increase their chances for marital success—unless this big step is preceded by an even bigger step: an engagement to be married. So many marriage counselors are now saying it might be better not to live together, where you get close enough to find out that you cannot live with your partner's faults but have become too close and too entangled to make an easy exit and live without that partner.

If you take nothing else from this chapter, take this: X types and Y types interpret living together very differently. Many Y type men have reemphasized their single status even as they were moving their furniture into their girlfriend's house—yet those girlfriends were still glowing in the excitement of their boyfriend's new commitment.

Contact is Contract

We've talked about how Y types treat the words of their X partners as a binding contract, but for X types, physical contact certainly initiates their contract. Take Sylvia's case. She was in a relationship with an attorney for two years but took an entire year before allowing things to get physical. I knew Sylvia but never met her boyfriend, so I couldn't say with certainty what his personality type was. But after a year of being extremely intimate, Sylvia was in love. She spoke to me about talking to him about a commitment, about taking the relationship to the next level. I was a bit worried. I felt he would have broached the subject if he was ready to do so. He didn't strike me as the shy type. I was beginning to smell a rat or a vole, and it seemed to be a mountainous Montane vole to me. But, Sylvia needed to discover this on her own. On their two-year "anniversary," they went out to dinner and she asked him to be exclusive with her. He bluntly said "No!" She asked for an explanation.

He said, "I just don't want to."

She complained, "But you've been intimate with me for a year. Are you seeing someone else?"

He replied, "You know there's no one else. But I think we should drop this topic before someone gets hurt."

"I'm a big girl," she snapped back. "I can take it. Tell me!"

"Well, I just don't see you as the type I would marry."

"What!" she screamed. "But I'm good enough to sleep with? For a whole year?"

He just shrugged his shoulders and turned his head, and uttered something inaudible.

Several self-help books suggest that women should abstain for three months because guys who are "dogs" (not serious) won't waste that much time on one, when they could have had 12 or more conquests during that same time period. Would that advice have worked for Sylvia? She abstained for 12 months and still, not even a commitment.

To Ys reading this chapter, you need to know that to X types, contact…is a contract. Many men and women in their twenties, and most teenagers, are not ready for marriage, and if you're an X in that age range, it's safe to assume that your love interest is *not* interested in the same things you are. Remember those rodents in our last chapter? The researchers conducted an experiment to see whether it was necessary for monogamous voles to have sex to bond for life. So they put several females in cages next to single, unattached males. Remember what they found? We touched on this before. They found that after spending time together, most of them became couples for life, bonded by the closeness—sometimes by the touch *through* the wire, but not by sex, which was impossible because of the wire that separated them.

You do not need to sleep with your friend to keep him or her; in addition, from a biochemical standpoint, becoming sexual, produces no guarantees because you won't know whether your partner bonds in this way.

Sylvia's "boyfriend" enjoyed her sexually. He probably wasn't promiscuous because of fear of contracting a disease, but it wasn't real monogamy. What was a nonverbal contract for her was simply a pleasurable, long-term contact for him. It's also important to know that oxytocin, the bonding agent, begins to flow long before the sex act begins. It can be turned on by touching, by talking, by scent. It's really no good to *play*—if you're planning to *prey* on someone and use them recreationally. This is the one time that I always encourage Ys to stick with their own kind. After all, you just might escape the drama that is almost certain to come from a wounded X.

The YY type woman is probably able to take anything you can pull out of your bag of tricks, and needing to eventually "abandon" your emotional X types will just complicate your game.

I can be clearer. If your motives in love are superficial or temporary, then X type partners should be the last people on your bucket list. This is not to say that Ys don't need or want true love, too. This is only a message to the select few Ys who know from the start that their intent is to have a good time physically, rather than settle down permanently.

Why X's Withhold Sex when Angry

I almost feel that by now, you can give me the answer to this one. You probably would have read this a little differently in other books. Other self-help books using the old paradigm, the old way of thinking, would have titled this as, "Why *Women* Withhold Sex when Angry." In chapter 1, I urged you to reinterpret studies and books along XY lines instead of gender lines, correcting the stereotype. Simply apply XY theory to it. Wherever you see a generalization about men and women, assume that by "men" they mean "Ys" and by women, they mean "Xs." Still, as I mentioned before, this may not seem fair to men; several men who discovered they were X types were suddenly afraid of being feminized. Nothing is further from the truth.

There are female Y's just as there are male Xs, and that is nothing to be ashamed of. One scientist, in an attempt to explain what we now know using XY theory, explained it this way. "Sometimes, for no apparent reason, male components get misplaced and are found in females, while female parts…" You get where this is going? In fact, you may not because I didn't when I first read it. It might have been put somewhat indelicately. The author was not referring to genitalia. He was attempting to highlight the fact that, what was stereotypically true of women just decades ago, simply is no longer true today.

And the same goes for men. So, let's get back to why women (I mean Xs) don't enjoy being asked for sex when they are angry, worried, or dealing with some form of conflict. Being angry would never be a reason for a Y type to cancel plans to play golf or mow the lawn, just as being angry won't cancel a woman's plans to go home and cook dinner for her children. But sex, on the other hand, communicates that everything is OK.

As you guessed, though sex is an activity shared by two, it's a different type of sharing for the X than it is for the Y. It's an act of bonding for Xs, who would not want to be that close to someone they're fighting with, and duty and responsibility have nothing to do with it. This is difficult for Y types to grasp who may be quick to point out that your anger didn't prevent you from cooking the family dinner, feeding the pets, or putting the children to bed—so why does sex get axed? We mentioned earlier that Ys view sex as a service or duty that a partner provides, or as just another shared activity. This explains some of their confusion when sex is withheld in trying, emotional times.

But if you're an X, it's important to consider the flip side as well. Ys see your "acts" or "actions" as a demonstration of love. Remember? "Actions speak louder than words." Withholding sex could be interpreted as a signal of a change in emotions, rather than as a temporary break in your feelings of connectedness. The Y's worry here is premature, but we can all agree that if this withholding is occurring often, and over a long period of time, feelings can indeed begin to wane on both sides, and the marriage could be in jeopardy. So the sexual contract may need reconsidering and rewriting by X types.

Several books have covered the fact that many "men" only become affectionate hours before they plan to solicit sex from their partners. I need to let you know, "men," that you're not that subtle. They're on to you, and they don't like it one bit. Even if you're a Y type male, wouldn't it just be smarter to start buttering her up a bit earlier? Like the day before?! Quit being so transparent. It's not that hard. Talk and touch. Talk and touch. Some conversation, a little affection, and some help around the home. That is where your X type partner gets the oxytocin to put her in the mood—not just two hours before you put the kids to bed. One husband buys his wife roses every Friday evening to ensure he'll have a good weekend. The roses won't wither before Monday, and if any anniversaries or birthdays fall in between, he's covered. It still is a chemical affair.

Hurt People, Hurt People

I must admit, I got the above caption from one of my clients. He explained to me that he was dating out of his league. Mark had landed himself a model when, by way of appearance, he considered himself average at best. If you don't believe that the market value you place on yourself, as well as how your lover views and values herself, is a spoiler (a variable that can alter the application of XY theory), then be sure to read all the way through to the last chapter.

Mark's girlfriend kept disappearing and reappearing. He explained that his hurt feelings nose-dived into a depression when he learned that his girlfriend was, in fact, dating his own brother behind his back. When he confronted her for an explanation, she explained that a cousin had done the same thing to her over five years ago, and since then, she had never been able to seriously care about the feelings of anyone, particularly the men who were "foolish enough to date" her (her words). Then she ended with this winner: "So you see, Jack (his name was Mark), what I'm trying to say is that "Hurt People, Hurt People!"

It is interesting to note that at the Institute, it seemed that Ys, by their own confessions, had a more difficult time getting over past hurts and were more likely to hurt partners in future relationships for the wrongs done to them in previous relationships. I typically advise my Xs who are determined to date Ys to ask them if they have been hurt in the past, how often, and how recently. It also would help to ask them how many women or men they could say they truly loved. Their answer to that question will give you perspective.

Xs have quite the opposite problem—of not holding past hurts in long-term memory in order to learn from them; as a result, they are prone to repeat their mistakes in dating the same personality type. It was this tendency that prompted me to write a *Workbook for XY Couples* as a companion to the XY theory I and II, where both Xs and Ys could record their experiences and work through their differences using XY tips and techniques. For those not currently in a relationship, the XY Workbook for Singles will provide the tools to assist them in finding someone that matches their personality type.

Strip Clubs, Pornography, and Prostitution

Strip clubs have become quite the rage for many, and not just for unmarried males. Even some married clergy have confessed to these addictions. Whether X or Y types, rich or poor, secular or religious, these clubs are more often frequented by men than by women. With the age of the Internet, pornography and prostitution have all been on the rise. It's obvious that men who are, by nature, more visual would be drawn to these practices, but I had an interesting thought one day as I listened to a couple who came in for XY testing; they argued about his visits to strip clubs and the fact that he had also considered legal prostitution and was a frequent viewer of online pornography. He kept trying to present his case to his wife that he's "not interested in those girls" and that "his love for her remained unchanged." Whether coming from a politician caught with his pants down or from some unfortunate John in a police sting operation, the defense is not new. The guilty often continue to pledge their undying support for their partner while clinging to their practices as merely recreational.

It would seem that wives, interested in keeping their husbands' interest sexually, could do more than promise to be a "whore" in bed, as the saying goes. I believe, in addition to the variety and the excitement and newness that Ys especially enjoy, what makes strippers and prostitutes alluring is the fact that they allow for emotional distance. They usually won't want to know your name, nor will they tell you theirs. They're there to provide a "service," and you don't have to worry about cuddling after or the affection and small talk before. It is a shared "activity," a service. It's nothing more than a dopamine rush.

But let's not rush to minimize the problem. A recent study showed that the self-esteem of women often takes a hit once they discover their man is a serial pornographer. The reasons are simple. Most wives believe they will not look as good as porn stars or ever have everything in such perfect propor-tions. They feel that if they were enough for their men, these partners wouldn't need their Internet thrills. It's hard to argue against that, even if I pointed out that many men who *are* looking for what they believe are harmless thrills would never "hook up" with a stripper or porn star if given the opportunity and often continue to love their wives and want to be in the relationship.

Arguments such as these are even more difficult to sup-port, though, when research indicates that many men have admitted that over time, their attraction to their partners declined with the heavy use of porn, and the proclivity for pornography increased to the point of addictions in some. However, I can share the difference in how X types and Y types viewed the problem. Y type men more often blamed their behavior on the following:

1. Duty. Their partner's failure to perform their "sexual" duty. They felt sex shouldn't have been put on the negotiation table when problems arose, even if "she" thought she was tired and overworked domestically. In this vein, another more control-ling Y male who would never let his wife off the hook said, jokingly, "She'll do it with me, and she'll like it!"

2. Frequency. Clearly, any drop in the frequency of sex is a problem for men, particularly Y type, testosterone-filled men. We've advised couples to talk honestly about expected sexual frequency because libidos vary from person to person regardless of personality type. It helps to keep in mind that a lack of equity in domestic chores—and the stress and resentment that follow—are enough to wipe out the sex drive of the disadvantaged partner, whether male or female.

3. Novelty. Some Y type men wanted an Olympic medal for satisfying their need for novelty and variety by resorting to strip clubs and online porn. After all, they weren't touching anyone or doing anything wrong. They were satisfying their needs remotely, instead of cheating. As much as this view is infuriating to women, we've encouraged our X types to add as much variety to the bedroom activities as possible. Without the luxury of oxytocin bonding, Y types also reported boredom more often. One Y man explained that his wife would never dream of preparing a potato salad for *every* single meal without expecting the family to soon get tired of it, so why would she expect that attitude to work in bed?

We managed to convince this man before he left the Institute that variety in sex is not the exclusive responsibility of women. Unlike meals served from the kitchen, he did not have the right to wait to be served!

4. Visual Effects. We credit the following insights to the bluntness of Y type males. But many explained that they turned to pornography because their wives no longer looked the way they had when first married—or before they had their children. Fair? Probably not. But wives in XY relationships are under more pressure to monitor and manage weight gain and general overall appearance because Y types tend to place more focus on superficial variables. One Y male shared his bias in front of his wife, who immediately pointed out that she didn't sign up for his "pot belly or the love handles around his gut," either.

Remember Dr. Zak's research in his book *The Moral Molecule*? Give-and-take type reciprocation is not a trait of those short on oxytocin. Don't expect your Y type partner to see the fairness of staying in good physical shape if the same is being expected of you. This is likely to be a circular argument that never ends, never gets resolved in an XY relationship.

5. Emotionality. This was not a direct observation of Y males but rather our conclusions drawn from the Y type personality and their other comments about why they were drawn to people they weren't married to.

Strip clubs were attractive to Ys because there was no emotional expectation. So, our advice to X type partners was that they should suck the emotions out of their sexual encounters with their partner, if only for the sake of providing variety. Yes, this would feel more like role play for you, but quite thrilling to him. Be as detached and aloof as he would expect a strange woman on the street to be. It obviously wouldn't hurt to offer things he would never have expected to receive. Don't say those I love you's during lovemaking with a Y. Instead, withhold them. No cuddling before. No cuddling after. Be matter-of-fact. No sentimentality. Sometimes you will find that a little emotional vacuuming can carry a marriage and an XY relationship a long way.

Chapter 14

Sculpting and Changing

The Michelangelo Effect

*S*ome time ago, researchers identified a phenomenon that plays a role in couples falling in love. Known as the self-expansion model, its effect is quite often seen in early stages of dating (couples) when, according to one study, individuals in a relationship begin with hopes of learning new and exciting things. This discovery leads to the feeling of falling in love. The influencing of each other, the sharing communicatively, and the willingness to experience each other's activities together are all so pronounced that a researcher in Amsterdam (now deceased) dubbed the effect the Michelangelo Effect. The term is used to describe the way new lovers shape each other's behavior and "sculpt" each other in ways that enable each partner to meet his or her personal goals in the relation-ship. Dr. Hyman, author of *How to Know If It's Time to Go*, listed the 2-year mark as the first of three points in a marriage when couples are at high risk for breaking up. The other two are the 12-year mark, when family time is used to get the kids to soccer and Little League, and the "empty nest" period after 20 years of marriage, when kids have left their parents alone to their own self-discoveries.[36]

But back to the first marker. If we don't figure out what is happening at this early stage, we won't need to worry about the empty nest. Most people show up to first dates with their date representatives and not their true personas. Rather, who-ever you believe your new interest wants to see is who you will present. We called this "functional faking"; and although some Y type men believe this type of lying serves a justifiable func-tion at this point, these are not always "white lies". More than a few X type women have complained about men who lied about not smoking even one cigarette their entire lives, and then a year or two into the relationship, a chain smoking habit is unearthed. Why would someone lie about verifiable facts such as the following: How many kids do you have? Have you been married before? Do you pay child support and take care of your children? Do you have any vices—a drinking problem, drug use, psychological disorder? A "crazy" aunt, deranged uncle in the basement, a felony, no job?

X Delusion

It's not only Y type men who lie. Women have lied about children they hid at their parent's house, like flowers in the attic. They've also lied about drug use; credit problems, whether they really want kids or ever intended to go out to work. It's social lying and is as damaging as functional faking. But social lying is also typical of X's who lie to themselves about their ability to abide by their Y partners requirements, to adapt and change—only to find after years of "changing" the core of their being that there was never a Michelangelo Effect for two.

Carlos got the shock of his life when he flew out to Orlando, Florida, to propose to a woman he had been dating over the Internet for nine months. The day after he placed a four-thou-sand-dollar ring on the lady's finger, he found out she did not own a house in Orlando like she had said. It was her mother's. She did not have the permanent job she claimed; she had been placed by a temp agency in a job that she serendipi-tously lost the day before he proposed to her. She did lose 30 pounds like she told him, but she did not tell him that she had done so with lap band surgery that in her instance resulted in complications that would affect her quality of life for years to come.

Change We Can Believe In?

Remember Joe and his girlfriend with eyes like a doe? She was the girl who liked all the things that Joe liked. She said all the right things. Loved the movies he loved. Remember how he jumped into that relationship so fast that friends cautioned him to be careful? Well the only thing that remained a reality were her beautiful eyes and her accent. Everything else changed. She no longer said all the right things. In fact, she said many things that were wrong and hurtful, and said these things over and over. Joe felt pushed away by the nagging and withdrew. Well, when the dust of euphoria settled, she realized she didn't like all the movies Joe was fond of. In fact Joe found out she didn't enjoy going to the movies at all. Their taste in music? As far from each other's as the East is from the West.

His favorite music was *not* on her iPod™. It wasn't even on one of the programmed stations in her car. She said she wanted two kids because he did, but then admitted to him later that she really wanted four kids, but wanted to please him so much she actually believed she could settle for two. They both gave the relationship their all, and for some time she even succeeded in pretending to be the conversationalist that she was not. What had gone wrong? When they got together, the chemicals producing the excitement and butterflies in the stomach convinced her that she could change her personal taste and preferences. But she couldn't sustain the effort beyond the honeymoon stage. She got tired of forcing herself to be who she was not. She had a high intimacy score, so she talked a lot—about emotions only and about their relationship—but casual conversation was lacking. Joe was so moved by her verbal promises to follow him to the ends of the earth, her promises of undying support, that he never noticed that casual conversation was completely missing.

They gave their relationship their best shot but failed after 18 months. Here is the dangerous delusion in XY relationships. When Y types and X types meet, Y types practice what we described as functional faking; they're aware that what they're saying is not the entire truth and that the romance they're bringing is not sustainable, but the end justifies the means for them. Especially if at the end of their efforts, they convince their X types that what they see is what they're actually getting. After your heart is theirs, they can quit bringing the roses, paying for dinners, cooking your special meals, and being attentive to you and the children—even quit being quite so respectful and agreeable.

This is not change. They are now being who they always were. You were just "faked" out, or deceived. This is their *dangerous deception* and you, their unknowing victim.

But what about X types? If you're a classic X type, yours is the *dangerous delusion*: self-delusion. Because, at the very beginning of the relationship, some Y's, who are more forthcoming, would have told you, "I am who I am, and you'll have to take me as I am."

Xs, however, delude and deceive themselves into believing that they can adjust to the many demands and idiosyncrasies of their partner. Indeed some can. But Joe and his doe could not. She found she couldn't sustain the changes and gave up completely, forcing them both to completely abandon the relationship.

Would the XY Relationship Personality Test have either helped their relationship or saved them from each other and the painful tears these two lovers both shed?

The Michelangelo Effect can often last as long as two years or more, but this is not very likely for XY couples. With classic Xs needing conversation, interaction, affection, and reassurance to bond—and Y type partners being unable to supply these indefinitely—problems are sure to ensue.

The result is that both partners will feel that they made a mistake when the faking stops, the delusion ends, and the relationship is placed in serious jeopardy. The secret is to bridge the gap on the continuum. Each partner must make a commitment to nudge himself or herself along the XY continuum—in the direction of their partner—to become what that partner portrayed in the beginning. The non-talking Y must force himself to show some verbal interest in the affairs of his wife. His X type wife must also do her part and edge along on the continuum—by talking less if needed—so as not to overwhelm her man with words that force his need for solitude and space. Reciprocation in an XY relationship becomes more critical because individuals appear to be intentionally holding back on what is required and needed to foster bonding between both partners.

Should You Stay?

One girl I knew dated a guy who wouldn't commit for issues of trust. Benjamin drank a lot and was a commitment-phobe—committed only to living one day at a time. Barbara was a church-going protestant. No profanity. Healthy eating. Exercising religiously. After "Ben" however, she now drank heavily, curses like a fisherman, and has become a nervous wreck due to Ben being Ben. She got the silent treatment, often. Disappearing acts. And no reciprocity of her love or care. Classic behavior of his cohort—Y type males. Then he told her that if she didn't like it, she could leave. But it was, after all, her apartment.

What If There's A Personality Disorder (one of the spoilers)?

Someone asked this at the Institute. This is an excellent question. As we mentioned earlier, the XY test is about compatibility of a relational nature. If you're in an XX relationship, you should have peace, joy, and a hopeful future if you have at least some major things in common. But what if you discovered only six months into the marriage that he or she has a bipolar disorder or a borderline personality disorder? Either of these problems are serious enough to "spoil" or interfere with what would be the natural and expected outcome in XY theory. Stay with me, I'm going somewhere with this. According to the DSM IV, the diagnostic manual used by psychologists, therapists, and psychiatrists to determine their clients' mental health status, these are the symptoms of someone with BPD: real or imagined fears of abandonment; personal attacks toward any family or friend they love; unstable and intense interpersonal relationships; mood swings that affect you directly; intense anger, outbursts, and difficulty controlling emotions and thoughts; and often some obsessive compulsive behavior. He or she lashes out at you in the most mean way physically or verbally. Those around him or her feel that they must walk on eggshells to avoid causing some offense because those with BPD are often hypersensitive to perceived wrongs. The version of this disorder that is more prevalent in men is known as antisocial personality disorder, but many of the relationship destroying symptoms are the same.

Question: Would you desert your spouse on the basis of what she can do or say to hurt you emotionally? Before you answer, keep this in mind—her condition is no fault of her own, she did not ask for, or contribute in any way to having this aspect of her personality. Some of you might not run away. But some studies have shown that the condition is not helped by the high oxytocin production that accompanies the tenderness, compassion, and touchiness that an emotional X needs and also gives. Being with someone with this condition might be more difficult for you, if you are the naturally more sensitive X. So would you leave or would you stay?

Let Me Introduce You to X Type Guilt

Three young women were to marry enterprising young men from their hometown in Nairobi, Kenya. The first two followed the script and chose men from their hometown. But, the third woman chose someone from the United States. This third woman had problems even before the Michelangelo Effect could go into effect. She was an XX type. The one thing she needed was the very thing her husband could not offer;

intimacy. (I don't know what the problem is with these guys. Intimacy should be the easiest to fake functionally.)

I had another client in an XY relationship who wanted to know what to do. I was curious to know if my friend from Nairobi would have any advice for my client. So, I asked her. And she did. She said, "I have been married for 20 years now and have cried myself to sleep for 19 of those years. It's really my fault...I was used to meeting guys who were XX or YY, so when my current husband came across as an X (in communication only), I truly assumed he was an XX type who was holding back his affection because he was very religious— so 'my bad.' I guess I was wrong. It's not all bad. I've finally stopped crying; I would still give a kidney for a hug though. But I must admit, he is a good provider, he's faithful, and he helps me in functional ways. Tell your friend she is in for a very long, miserable life. If he is a YY and she's not, there is no hope. Before my husband, I dated a YY and dumped him after a month. If she could, she should do the same."

But to this day, Cassaundra, the advice giver, is still with her husband. When I inquired why, she said quite simply, "Guilt. You must be sure your conscience can withstand the guilt imposed on you and worsened by family and friends who won't sympathize with a black woman stepping out on a successful black man, who in this country is an endangered species. A man who has never cheated on me, abused me, or the children."

Cassaundra insisted that the hug is symbolic of many other intimate things and that what she really complains about is having her emotional needs treated as trivial.

The Value Differential

We've found a formula of sorts that requires more research but seems to work so far. We call it the Value Differential. Some scientists refer to this as "mate value." It involves your significant other giving you a rating from 1 to 10. We've found that when Y's are asked this question, they often resort to superficial variables to define you (i.e., for Y men: how much weight you gained, or how "hot" you are, or how pretty you are; for Y type women: how secure you are financially, or how tall you are, or how good you are sexually).

X types tend to be more global in their rating. So the X type woman might say: He's not that good-looking, but he treats me well and takes care of his children, and I love him. I'll rate him 8/10. He gets a better "mate value" rating from his X-type wife.

So our value index (the Value Differential) has a global score to force someone to rate the overall package—and a "heat index" to determine how "hot" you think you are compared to your partner. The partners with the highest self-rating relative to their partners expected the most and changed the least. The partners with the lower rating put up with more of their partners' flaws and adjusted or changed more. Equal ratings often led to fair and equitable treatment, which is why so many self-help experts advise you to date at your level of good looks, class, education, intelligence, and so forth, as much as possible. If you could find out the truth about how your partner rates you compared to how he rates himself, you would have all the answers you'd ever need about the possibility of change. But, we'll cover more of this in book two of the XY theory.

Before You Began

My wish for you is love and happiness and the quality of life you want and deserve. I trust your judgment, your ability to look objectively at the entire body of evidence we've presented, and what your partner presents to you—and that you will do what is best for *you*. One woman said that after considering the XY theory, she was convinced her husband did not have a shred of love or affection for her. She was an X and he, a Y. But she wouldn't leave him for another man because she couldn't trust herself to not make the same decision, or a choice considerably worse. This way, though she was indescribably sad, her 4 kids didn't know it, and at least they had their real dad, she explained.

I felt bad for them. But they didn't have what you now do— the knowledge that the number of Y type women and caring-loving X type men out there (who often make great stepdads) is rising every day. A seismic shift in the makeup of our society is underway, and there are more X men and Y type women out there than ever before. She didn't have to stay, and if she left, she didn't have to repeat her mistake. You, however, know better. You now know about XY theory. You know whether your personality profile is XX, XY, YX, or YY and you know what to look for so that you find someone who's right for you. Certainly someone with high needs for communication would be better suited for someone who enjoys communicating— from simple things like saying "good morning" or "good night" to asking you how your day was, to being able to freely tell you how much he cares.

The man with higher emotional needs—who enjoys affec-tion, touching and hearing how much his partner loves him— won't be happy with a Y type person who thinks emotional expression and sharing show "neediness." You now know how to spot Y type personalities a mile off. Clues abound— from their style of communication, with their short texting—all the way to the self-centered content of their conversation and interests. Or their unwillingness to want to chat, help, or hang out in an attempt to make you happy, to meet *your* needs. In book two, we'll focus on what to do if you're already in an XY relationship and how to deal with the control issues, conflict and lack of compromise that such relationships bring. I will show you how to change a rigid partner or if you're in-between relationships, how to change your approach to dating so you attract those who can truly meet your needs.

My friend doesn't have to repeat her mistake. Looking back, she could now easily see a dozen warning signs she missed before. I'll cover these in the next book.

The unhappy, unsatisfying familiar is not better than the potentially fulfilling unknown. But, if like her, you too decide to stay with who you've got, then I'll show you what you need to do to make the necessary adjustments to keep the love of your life. Either way, I wish you the very best, and I thank you for taking the first half of this journey with me.

Before You Leave

*N*ow that you know what I know about XY Theory and how it affects our relationships, I can tell you about the tools we have prepared to help you to cope with life in the new XY world you're about to encounter. These tools are discussed in the book, XY Theory Volume II, which will be available in a few months.

For couples, a 14-week online program is free for those who have purchased this book from our website, XYTheory. com. It isn't uncommon for one partner to be unwilling to seek help from a therapist or other trained professional for relation-ship issues. Our online program for XY couples brings the help you need —to you—right on your phone, your laptop or tablet.

For singles or those in between relationships, you'll notice your world has changed too, along with everyone in it. You're now surrounded by Xs and Ys and mixed XY personalities.

Our online program will help you to date differently and seek matchups with those who can truly make you happy. This online Workshop for Singles is free if you purchased the book, XY Theory on our website.

We've also found that those who journal their new discoveries benefit more from writing down their ideas. So for couples, we have designed a workbook, The Interactive Workbook for XY Couples™, which will allow you to work on the differences that drive you apart and wreak havoc in your relationship.

For singles and those starting over, our workbook titled, Before You Begin (Again)™ – An XY Workbook for Singles, will help you take a closer look at how you date and enable you to better re-position yourself for dating success.

Both workbooks will be available in the spring of 2013.

Visit us at XYTheory.com. We will guide you every step of the way and provide you with a free forum to share your experiences with personalities just like yours. See you there!

ENDNOTES

Chapter 1: How Relationships End before They Begin

[1] The Jacob Research Institute™ was established to conduct research on the many applications of XY theory. Initially, our primary goal was to discover the one trait or factor that best predicts whether couples would succeed or fail. It became evident to our team that XY theory affected the way we do business, the way we form relationships, even the way we vote or choose careers. New applications are being discovered every day. Visit us at www.JacobResearchInstitute.com.

[2] The XY Personality test™ is the instrument used to assess one of four personality types that predict compatibility in a relationship. X types differ from Y types who often revel in their solitude, show less tolerance for a poor relationship, but are also less likely to complain of loneliness when not in a committed relationship.

[3] Gottman, J. M. (1986). Dr. John Gottman joined the University of Washington's Department of Psychology and founded the Family Research Laboratory aka "The Love Lab."

[4] Bem, S. L. (1981). *Gender Schema Theory.* Masculinity and femininity should comprise "separate personality dimensions."

[5] Salt, B. (2012). *The Australian Newspaper.*

[6] De Angelis, B. (2001). *What Women Want Men to Know.* Leman, K. (2009). *Have a New Husband by Friday.* Sozio, D., & Brett, S. (2011). *The Man Whisperer.*

[7] Harvey, S. (2009). *Act Like a Lady, Think Like a Man.*

[8] Pease, B., & Pease A. (1998). *Why Men Don't Listen and Why Women Can't Read Maps.*

[9] Love, P., & Love, S. (2007). *How to Improve Your Marriage without Talking about It.*

[10] Jaynes, S. (2005). *Becoming the Woman of His Dreams.*

[11] Roy F. B. (2010). *Is There Anything Good About Men?*

[12] Gottman, J.M. (1999). *The Seven Principles for Making Marriage Work.* An escalation in negative communication, which deteriorates into criticism and finally contempt, was more destructive to the satisfaction of the couple.

Chapter 2: The Dangerous Need

[13] Brizendine, L. (2006). *The Female Brain*. There are hormones produced in the brain that make us want to bond, love, and connect with others.

[14] Maslow, A. (1954). The Hierarchy of Needs. *Motivation and Personality*. Food, shelter, etc, and then "safety" and "security" are some of the basic lower-level needs of humans.

[15] *Oxford English Dictionary* (Second Edition ed.). (1989). *Astron*. Parallax is an "apparent displacement, or difference in the apparent position, of an object, caused by actual change (or difference) of position of the point of observation."

[16] Cain, S. (2012). *Quiet: The Power of Introverts in a World that Can't Stop Talking*.

Chapter 3: The X Type Personality

[17] Pease, B., & Pease, A. (1998). *Why Men Don't Listen and Why Women Can't Read Maps*. The Peases suggest that all boys are non-communicators who have used up their quota of words during the day at school and hence, are unwilling to communicate with family at home. Whereas, school girls with their inexhaustible supply of words, are more verbal and continue to converse normally when they get home.

[18] Brizendine, L. (2006). *The Female Brain.* The difference between the number of words that men and women used during their day.

[19] Mehl, M. (2007). Are Women Really More Talkative Than Men? *Science 317.*

Chapter 7: The Y Type Personality

[20] Tsapelas, I., & Aron, A., & Orbuch, T. (2009). Marital Boredom Now Predicts Less Satisfaction 9 Years Later. *Pshychological Science.*

Chapter 11: The Dangerous Test

[21] XYMatchQuest.com, a full and expanded version of the XY Personality test is available for compatibility testing and matchmaking.

[22] XY Theory Volume II. This volume helps you to identify if you already are in a relationship and covers topics common to XY couples such as how to deal with conflict, power struggles and control issues as well as compromise and change. Information is also shared to help singles to approach dating differently and only attract partners who can meet their needs.

[23] Allport, G. (1950; 1975). *The Nature of Personality: Selected Papers.* Gordon Allport was an American psychologist and one of the first to focus on the study of personality psy-

chology. Though he met with Sigmund Freud personally, he rejected the psychoanalytic approach to personality; he thought that more emphasis should be placed on an individual's present context than on his past.

[24] Maiden, R. J., Peterson, S. A., Caya, M., & Hayslip, B. R. (2003). Personality changes in the old-old: A longitudinal study. *Journal of Adult Development*, 10(1), 31-39. This study shows stability of Personality dimensions from the Big Five, spanning beyond young adulthood and into "old age", and interrupted only by changing life circumstances, so common to the elderly.

[25] McCrae, R., & Costa, P. T. (1987). Validation of the five-factor model of personality across instruments and observers. *Journal of Personality and Social Psychology, Vol 52(1), 81-90.*

[26] XYTheory.com and XYMatchQuest.com provide a means to have your personality computer scored, using algorithms that increase the accuracy of the test thereby eliminating a considerable amount of human error.

[27] X types in particular, find it helpful to "vent" or share their experiences with other X types in XY relationships. The website, XYTheory.com provides the forum that makes this type of sharing possible; however, the forum is not limited to just X types but is frequented by Y types as well.

[28] A free Workshop for XY Couples is provided on the internet for anyone who has purchased XY Theory books, Volumes I and II on XYTheory.com. The 14-week workshop improves interaction between partners.

Chapter 12: The Chemical Affair

[29] Young, L. (1994). See Dr. Young's website to follow his exciting research at http://research.yerkes.emory.edu/Young/larry.html. Dr. Young is a researcher in social attachment at Emory University in Atlanta, Georgia, at the Center for Behavioral Neuroscience. Young believes that prairie voles stay together because they get "a natural high" from being with their mates, while the Montane voles do not.

[30] Phelps, S.M., & and L.J. Young, L.J. (2003). Extraordinary diversity in vasopressin (V1a) receptor expression in wild prairie voles: Patterns of variation and covariation. *Journal of Comparative Neurology, 466:564-576.*

[31] Fisher, H. (2004). *Why We Love: The Nature and Chemistry of Romantic Love.* Fisher, a researcher at Rutgers University, contends that love comes in three stages, or levels, which we can participate in singularly or collectively.

[32] Zak, P.J. (2012). *The Moral Molecule: The Source of Love and Prosperity.*

[33] Weil, B. (1999). Understanding Adultery. *Make up, Don't Break Up: Finding and Keeping Love for Singles and Couples.*

Chapter 13: Putting the Y in Intimacy

[34] Harvey, S. (2009). *Act Like a Lady, Think Like a Man.* The reason Steve Harvey advised women to "date like a man" is simply that he presupposes that men, and men alone, know how to detach emotionally during intimacy.
[35] We do not conduct oxytocin experiments on humans or any other creatures, at The Jacob Research Institute, but we monitor all such studies closely and will keep you posted on our website, <u>www.JacobResearchInstitute.com</u>.

Chapter 14: Sculpting and Changing

[36] Birnbach, L., Hyman, B. (2010). *How to Know If It's Time to Go.*

Acknowledgments

So many have contributed to this book over the two years it took to write it. My brother Kent, my mother, and nephew offered their emotional support as no others could have.

But many friends freely shared their stories and experiences with me. To all of you, I offer my gratitude. Michelle, Cindy, Nancy G., Casaundra, Stacey, Lori, Lynette, Patty and Mo, Tammy, Valerie, Rosa, Jessica, Lori Hunt, Bonnie, Mike, Rachelle, Rachel, Khaleelah, Yvette P., Nancy Ross, Karen, Stormi, Jeff, Sellyna, Ndeye, Shirley, Michael B. Kelly II, Dr. Curtis A. Fox, Marc Rafael, Kimberly, Jenny, Gale, Angela, Ron, Ashley, Verna, Trish, Lauren R., Tania, Tamara, Claudia, Veronica, Casey, and Lori from Proofreadingpal.com

Dina, thank you for providing your unique brand of support and motivation. It worked!

Maria Rosales, Palwasha Alemzay, Dr. Carizma Chapman, Richard, Monique, Jigna, Natalia, Nichole, and the entire crew at The Jacob Research Institute, thank you. You're the real dream team!

Yvette Ayuso, you had the last lap in this relay, and you handled the rushed preparations and last-minute changes, commendably. Thank you for your selfless, timely contributions.

CPSIA information can be obtained at www.ICGtesting.com
Printed in the USA
LVOW132056010413

327087LV00001B/1/P